zydeco
ET PAS SALÉ

THE BEANS AREN'T SALTY :- CUISINE FROM SOUTH LOUISIANA
by Leonard Carter Hutchinson, BA, MFA, PHD

Published by
Zydeco's

Executive Chef + Author
Leonard Carter Hutchinson

Copy Editor
Courtney Leach

Creative Director
Kathy Davis

Text + Photography
Copyright © 2011
Leonard Carter Hutchinson

Copyright © 2011
Gumbo Ya Ya, Inc.

Food photography
Copyright © 2011
Charles Park

All rights reserved. No part of this book may be reproduced in any form without written permission from the publisher.

ISBN: 978-0-615-47029-0

10 9 8 7 6 5 4 3 2 1

Zydeco's
11 East Main Street
Mooresville, Indiana 46158

www.zydecos.net

CONTENTS

Foreword, 4

Back to Basics
The Trinity, 13
Mirepoix, 13
Basic Roux, 14
Stock Facile (Easy Stock), 15
Brown Stock, 15
Duck Stock, 15
Shrimp Stock, 15
Hollandaise, 16
Mayonnaise, 16
Crawfish Sauce a la Thibodaux, 16
Remoulade, 16
Jus Lie (Simple Sauce), 17
Alphreadeaux, 17
Espagnole Sauce, 17
Marchand de vin Sauce (The Wine Merchant's Sauce), 17
Béchamel, 17
Bordelaise a la Mouvrelle Onleans, 17
Béarnaise Rouge (Red Béarnaise), 18
Meuniere, 18
Zydeco's Shrimp Sauté, 18

Sausages and Seasoning Meats
Andouille, 23
Boudin, 25
Chaurice, 27
Boutte Alligator Sausage, 29
Tasso, 31
Pickled Meats, 33

Sunday Brunch
Crawfish Tasso and Chaurice Omelet with Shredded Pepper Jack Cheese, 37
Oyster and Chicken Liver En Brochette with Sweet Mirliton Spears and New Orleans Bordelaise (Angels and Devils on Horseback), 39
German Coast Boudin with Onions, Beer and Creole Mustard Pan Sauce, 41
Shrimp Sauté with Fried Grit Cakes and Béchamel Sauce, 43
Café Nouvelle Orleans, 44
Broiled Frog Legs with Crab Ravigote, Asparagus and Creole Tomato, 45
Andouille and Potato Galette with Braised Cabbage, 47
Lost Bread, 49
Sazerac, 51
Hurricane, 51
Cherry Bounce, 53
Absinthe, 53

Old Square
Golden Alligator Sauce Piquant, 57
Crawfish Pie, 59
Red Beans and Rice with Sausage, 61
Seafood Gumbo, 63
Shrimp Creole, 65

Fish and Seafood
Catfish Pecandine and Dirty Rice with Blood Orange Olive and Red Onion Salad, 69
Fried "Bustah" Crabs with Tomato and Avocado Remoulade, 71
Shrimp Baronne, 73
Speckled Trout Stuffed with Catfish, 75
Blackened Red Snapper with Chipotle Aioli, Tiger Shrimp Creole Sauce and Hammered Brussels Sprouts, 77

Fat Tuesday
Crawfish Boil, 83
Les Chevrettes Boucane Boutte (BBQ Shrimp), 85
Crab, Artichoke and Garlic Pizza, 87
Beignet L'ecrevisse, 89
Muffulettas with Gaufrettes, 93
Peacemakers with Horseradish Aioli, 95
Buffaleaux Wings with Creole Cream Cheese and Pickled Mirliton, 97
Oreilles Sales (Pigs Ears 3 Ways), 99
Duck and Andouille Jambalaya, 101

Pasta
Blackened Crab Cakes in a Nest, 105
North Shore Duck and Tasso Pasta, 107
Jolie Blon Pasta, 109
Madame Chiffonade (Rag Pasta), 111

Meats
Beef Tenderloin Au Poivre Piquant with Béarnaise Rouge, 115
Pecan-Encrusted Crawfish and Gruyère-Stuffed Lamb Chops with Orange Reduction Mirliton Slaw and Grilled Eggplant, 117
Pork Debris Boule with Garlic Potato Smash (The Monreauxvia), 118
Tassoed Pork Tenderloin and Potato Nanoose with Onion and Kumquat Gastrique, 121
Panèed Meat and Broiled Oysters with Roasted Beets, Poached Egg and Chevre, 123
Smoked Chicken Ya Ya with Crawfish Maque Choux and Sweet Potato Chloe, 125
Chicken Pontalba with Mirliton, Mission Figs and Red Rice, 127
Duck Clemenceaux, 129
Duck Abbeville with Creole Salpicon, Carrot, Onion and Turnips, 131

Desserts
Beignets with Café Au Lait, 135
Pecan Pie with Coffee and Chicory Whipped Cream, 137
Chocolate and Coffee Doberge with Drunken Rum Bananas and Pecans, 139
Blueberry and White Chocolate Bread Pudding with Chambord Sauce, 141

Index, 142

Carter "Hutch" Hutchinson moved to Indiana after meeting his wife Deb, an Indiana native, during Mardi Gras in 1996.

THE FOREWORD
HOW TO SUCCEED IN THE RESTAURANT BUSINESS DESPITE YOURSELF

My educational background is as chaotic as our restaurant, Zydeco's. I was trained in the fine arts – graphic design, art history, aesthetics, painting, ceramics – and in computer science – artificial intelligence, pedagogy and programming with a smidgen of electrical and nuclear engineering thrown in for good measure. I've had enough painting courses to choke Picasso, enough drawing courses to stun Miro, enough art history to drown Jansen and just over two decades dealing with computers in one form or another.

My Sister-in-law gave me a T-shirt imprinted with the clever missive, "College was the best 12 years of my life." The joke is that it wasn't a joke. I was in college for 12 years, either unwilling or incapable of deciding what to do with myself. That, paired 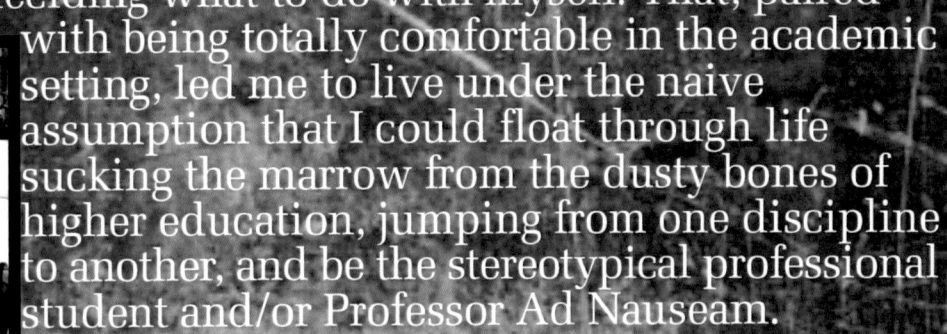 with being totally comfortable in the academic setting, led me to live under the naive assumption that I could float through life sucking the marrow from the dusty bones of higher education, jumping from one discipline to another, and be the stereotypical professional student and/or Professor Ad Nauseam.

While in school, I took short detours and on occasion dropped in on the real world. One of my most notable jobs was at a nuclear power plant in Louisiana, which for legal reasons, I will not name here. It's a big, impressive mother reactor, active and despite me, working still. Yes, that's right, I was a sort of Homer Simpson with a half-ass French accent, a radioactive Jerry Lewis dubbed in Louisiana patois and let me tell you, that plant scared the crap out of me.

A nuclear power plant is a reality of the most severe form and aspect. It is the opposite of the fine arts. It is the opposite of aesthetics. It is the opposite of beauty. It is cold and hard and absolute. It is physics of the most severe and unforgiving kind, and shit, I failed physics in college. I mean, that green glowing goo could really leave a nasty mark, something that's gonna hurt tomorrow, something that would certainly sting more than a paper cut if you weren't, like, stupid careful.

There are enough massive electrical things and sparks and rapidly moving sharp things and very loud smashing things and scary glowing things and silent but deadly things in a nuke plant to make Morgus the Magnificent jump up and down with glee, but not me. I used humor to mask my fear. I became quite the nuclear engineer/comedian, working the crowd, checking the instrumentation, sending out fake memos, activating a 20-ton valve, making rude sounds over the PA system, crawling through containment over the reactor core. "Thank you, thank you. Try the blackened steak and don't forget to tip your server. G'night, ladies and germs!" Yep, I was the life of the party, well liked by the higher ups and all seemed well. God, it was awful.

After a few years, I wanted to return to the comforting, insular and not nearly as dangerous world of the university, where most things wouldn't kill you if you accidentally bumped up against them. I used a letter of acceptance from a very well regarded institution of higher learning as my walking papers and got the hell out of Dodge as it were. But enough of that. The green-glowing stories I could tell you would make Edgar Allen Poe poop his pants. That's another book I'm gonna write one day (stories about the nuke plant, not Mr. Poe pooping in his drawz, for I have no firsthand knowledge of that).

Fast forward 1.2 decades, replete with some amazing highs and just as amazing lows. I scurried out the backdoors of some excellent educational institutions with three, cou[nt] 'em, three degrees. I also acquired a few trophies and a [sum] of money awarded to me on an artificial intelligence co[m]puter programming project I was working on at a famo[us] university in the South. I bring this up not to flaunt so[me] vast mega brain locked between my ears. (I certainly d[o not] possess that. Mega intelligence that is; I do have ears.) [But] perhaps an indication that I possess a modicum of stam[]ina, a touch of problem-solving ability, or at the very le[ast] I have some sort of gut feeling about certain things that matter to me in this life as I have come to know it.

But what does this have to do with a cookbook? Everything. For, despite my years training to become some so[rt] of Dungeons and Dragons mega-professor nuclear-ninja sage with three scrolls of wisdom, +50 hit points and a glowing flask of courage, I walked away from academia and the scary real world and went back to the thing I lo[ve] the most, the culinary arts. More specifically, the food a[nd] culture of my youth. I went back to basics. I went back [to] what was imparted to me through living most of my lif[e in] the greatest and most whacky place in the world. I look[ed] over my shoulder, back to the place where I was born: [New] Orleans. I reflected on a life immersed in that culture a[nd] decided to evoke its power and make it rise up as in the story line of some black and white 1950s horror movie [com]plete with dusty voodoo zombies and a mad scientist w[ith] a secret laboratory over an abandoned icehouse in the French Quarter.

A very famous chef once said that really great chefs [are] not artists but craft workers. They must turn out the same meal night after night with a degree of consistenc[y]. Well, you know, an assembly line robot with long spike[d] arms and fast spinning blades pretty much does that ve[ry] thing. It can deftly place tiny buzzing bits of uranium i[n] graphite tubes or, by loading in new software, extrude o[ut] a million big-butt mega-fat burgers with cheese or 11 bi[l]lion chicken nuggets, all of which are perfect clones, ea[ch] one to the other. Trust me, I know. I've had the misfortu[ne] of eating enough mechanically processed, chemically treated chicken bits in the last decade.

You might laugh at that, but just drive down any major street and see the depressing sight of fast food clone sit[es] that promise mind-numbing, tasteless conformity. It is [a re]ality of the most severe form and aspect. It is the oppos[ite] of the fine arts. It is the opposite of aesthetics. It is the o[p]posite of beauty. It is cold and hard and absolute. It is t[he] physics of the most severe and unforgiving kind, and sh[it] I failed physics. I mean, I grew up in a part of south Louisiana where food really is an art form. It is beautifu[l. It] is hot and sweaty and sticky, sexy, loud, messy and full [of] life. It has little claws and little feet and eyes and it was moving around just a second ago and now it's on your plate. It welcomes all and it's for everybody and it taste[s] damn good.

d the great fortune of spending a modicum of time traveling through Italy, from the northern city of Milan to ice to the south in Bari on the Adriatic Sea. I stayed h some great people and got to hang out in some fantas- kitchens. You could see the pride of the cooks with the wledge and techniques of generations past and I felt an ant connection. Great food comes from that. It's those y little secrets that those aloof chefs with the big hats the bad attitudes and the television shows, with the sing and the punching, don't want you to know. It's t you can easily cook great food, too.

t's what I'm talking about. I take what's in front of me with my super-ninja fine arts education and a nod to e-honored tradition, I approach the dish like it's a nting. I rely on fortuitous happenings, using a big ket of culture and the sage advice of thousands of souls ve never met, long gone to the back mists of history. I e my mother, my grandmother, my aunts and uncles ly whispering in one ear and the collective voice of a e and place on this planet in the other.

culinary career is as disjointed as Zydeco's 5, located eautiful downtown Mooresville, Indiana. I've been on ianapolis television deftly making BBQ shrimp at 6 lock in the morning and spewing out one-liners. I've to- y screwed up on private parties, costing Zydeco's much ney and pissing off many customers. I've had standing tions from the entire restaurant, which has literally ught me to tears, and I've had just as many irate cus- ers tell me just how much of an untalented hack I am. gotten a few awards, but I have fallen flat on my face re often. I've pushed enough jambalaya through the hen door of Zydeco's to choke Justin Wilson, enough kened steaks, medium, to stun Wolfgang Puck, enough wfish etouffée to drown John Folse and just over 10 rs dealing with the back end of the restaurant business ne form or another. That's how I cook. That's my life.

ce anything is etched in stone, it's dead. Don't believe ? When was the last time you heard anyone speak in? Why is English the big, bad voodoo language it is? It vived invasions from other tongues. It sucked up new rds, transformed old ones, made them better, mutated, ame leaner and meaner. It's alive and it can take on all ners. You can understand what I'm saying; you should getting a feel for who I am despite the dangling partici- s and the puckered conjunctives. The feeling is the im- tant thing, in life and in cooking.

n't get me wrong, there are certain things that you uld know before you attempt to invent the next great sine or new grammar rules in the Germanic languages. at's why you are reading this. That's what cookbooks are for. Learn a few of the basics presented here, expand your knowledge. The time-honored techniques are given to us for a reason: They just work. Who are we to fix something that is already damn good? Get to know them, use them, then break all the damn rules. Burn this book, fall on your face, let them say you are a hack, let the participles dangle, make that seafood gumbo yours. Be ready, though, cause I'm still gonna talk trash about it. That's my birthright. Then you've taken your first steps into cooking some good stuff. It's about luck. It's about pushing the limits. It's not about food that is sacred, no, no, no! It's about a food that is dynamic and alive and it can be great. That's a good thing. The dialogue keeps the culture alive and the food vibrant in a scary, robot food world.

So, within the pages of this book you should begin to see a pattern, a small taste as it were, of the traditions, the folklore, the customs, the view filtered and influenced through my eyes and my experiences set in a specific time and place. The why, the how, the technique to create some really great food. Louisiana cuisine is beautiful. It's hot and sweaty and sticky, sexy, loud, messy and full of life. It's eaten every day by beautiful people back home and around the world and it's my simple little gift to you.

Dear reader, respectfully submitted for your consideration this day, the 24th of February, 2009 in Morgan County, Mooresville, Indiana, USA.

39.612365 N
86.374362 W

Leonard Carter Hutchinson, BA, MFA, PhD
Zydeco's Cajun Actual

08

Creole-loving residents of Mooresville gather regularly to hear the musical stylings of bands like the Dan Holmes Gr... and Mojo Gumbo.

I love to cook and I love to watch people eat my food. so let me try to share with you a few New Orleans cooking secrets in book form.

BACK TO BASICS
SIMPLE CULINARY TECHNIQUES & RECIPES FROM SOUTH LOUISIANA (YOU'LL ROUX THE DAY)

You have your own agenda for being here. I, too, have one. Let's reveal mine first. I love to cook and I love to watch people eat my food. If you were here right now, I would make you something. It might be something I just made up or something with 100 years of history behind it. We might talk about nothing in particular or bemoan the sad state of the 21st-century culinary scene. We could discuss corporate American food or the flavors I've experienced in my travels through Europe. But mostly we would just cook and eat.

I love to read everything on the culinary arts. I listen to podcasts and Google about food incessantly. I wince at reality cooking shows, because I hate and love them. They remind me of the worst a kitchen can be. I am a voyeur. I have to watch. It all gets filed away somewhere in the naughty parts of my psyche.

As I am writing this, there are softshell crabs in the back sink. They are cruising around in a bowl with Mooresville's finest tap water flowing over them. The crabs are tonight's special, deep fried and served with tomato, avocado and remoulade,

I wish you were here so we could get drunk and try some little things guaranteed to impress your friends and family

and eaten whole. The recipe is old-school New Orleans, an entree greedily gobbled up by the natives back home.

Tonight, at the Z, I will sell about half of them. One customer will say they are the best thing ever, better than in the Crescent City. Another, not knowing of what they speak, will bitch that it tastes like crab(!?!), and the music is too loud, and they will just be a royal pain in the ass. As I like to say, "Everyone brings us pleasure here at The Z. Some when they come and others when they leave."

The kitchen hood is on. Because of an ominous structural steel beam propping up the second floor, the hood had to be placed way too low over the stove. I am continuously hitting my head on it and I have the bruises to prove it. For the past 10 years, my ears have been within inches of both the air intake and exhaust ducts, the sound of two large, three-phase motors drilling into my brain. This continuous high-decibel drone has made me a culinary Quasimodo, unable to hear anything but a constant ringing. It keeps me awake at night but damn it, the air is state approved and springtime fresh over that stove.

The fun continues. Just yesterday a man clutching a menacing metal clipboard strode through the back door, an official eagle and American flag on his car. He represented a certain recently created state agency. His job: Protecting us from evil-doers. He was also checking the greasiness of my stupidly low hood, the width of the wooden stairs and the length of the electrical cords splaying out from microwave ovens. Well, at some point my brain turned off and my eyes rolled into the back of my head. Using an impossibly small pencil, he was furiously scribbling into rows of perfectly straight rectangles, earnestly checking off boxes, performing essential duties, all for the safety of the citizens.

Here is a secret that is good to know if you ever start a restaurant: Beware of strangers with metal clipboards. They are made of a radioactive material from a red sun that will render a restauranteur helpless, a clerical Nosferatu with a nubby little pencil, a beaurocratic succubus that really, truly sucks. They are miniscule Napoleans and you hope it hasn't gone to their heads. Yes, beware of strangers holding metal clipboards in their little hands and a two-by-four up their posterior. They stand upon their massive tomes of byzantine rules written to confuse and obfuscate, others designed to quash anything you hope to accomplish. They invoke sections and subparagraphs as a voodoo priestess invokes secret incantations and then jabs a pin into a fetish. The bureaucrats are here to protect us from ourselves. Their intense earnestness is a pain in the ass. Usually that's where you feel the pin.

What does all this mean? It means I love to cook, and I put up with crap so I can do it for you. I will tolerate endless streams of metal clipboard nazis, clueless customers, employee no-shows. I will write this book for you, share my secrets with you, lose my hearing for you, get drunk with you. Because when it comes down to it, it's all about the food and hanging onto something great. The restaurant is just a means to that end. It's the most fun any one person should be allowed to have.

That's my agenda. I wish you were here so we could get drunk and try some things. I have cool stuff I've learned from other chefs, a train-wreck culinary reality show, Italy, a Web search or from my formative years in south Louisiana. It would be fun, but hard with me here and you displaced from me by time and space.

So let me try to give you a few secrets in book form, the analog version of a time machine that speaks to the future. Call up these, my ghost writings from the past. Read them with the covers pulled up over your head and a flashlight in hand, because this is going to get scary. When you're done, you will be just like me! Strike that. You will have taken a step on your culinary journey and you will be better than me. Stand on my shoulders and let me know what you see up there in the clean air. Just don't hit your head on the damn hood.

'MISE EN PLACE'
everything in its place

Chefs learn early that organization is vital. Before starting a recipe, read it over (twice to be sure), and get everything prepped. Measure out the spices and place them on little saucers. Have the meats ready in the refrigerator and any equipment close by. If needed, get the bain-marie on the stove and preheated. Have an instant-read digital thermometer and timer handy at all times. Invest in them, use mise en place.

THE TRINITY
or why I can't count to three

Many Louisiana recipes start with the trinity. It is the foundation onto which great food is built. It is simply diced onion, celery, bell pepper and, I would argue, garlic. Yes, I realize that's four things, but it's the trinity I use.

1 yellow or red onion, peeled, small dice
2 bell peppers, any color, seeded, medium dice
1 stalk celery, diced
1 toe garlic, diced

(makes about 2 cups)

When to use: Bean dishes, gumbos, jambalayas, Creoles, tomato sauce, smothered chicken, étouffées, braised meats

How to make it: Sauté in butter or oil until the onions become translucent. As the trinity cooks, add any seasonings to maximize flavor. The larger dice on the bell pepper means that it will still be visible in the final dish, a nice look. When braising, add 2 cups of uncooked trinity to the braising liquid.

How much to use: 2-4 cups on average

MIREPOIX

Generally, mirepoix is used in stocks, but some dishes call for this in place of a trinity. This recipe is as easy as it gets, but it adds wonderful flavor.

1 yellow or red onion, small dice
2 carrots, small dice
1 stalk celery, small dice

(makes about 2 cups)

When to use: With white beans, tomato sauce, stocks, soups, smothered chicken, braised meats

How to make it: For cooked mirepoix, sauté ingredients in butter or oil until the onions become translucent. As the mirepoix cooks, add any seasonings to maximize flavor. For raw mirepoix, add ingredients to braising liquids or with bones for a stock. Use with fresh thyme, bay leaf and parsley tied together in a little bundle (bouquet garni).

How much to use: 2-4 cups on average

THICKENING AND FLAVOR AGENTS

Roux (roo)

A roux is just oil and flour. It thickens liquidy, runny stuff, makes things shiny and adds flavor. It's really just oil and flour. Boy, does that sentence piss off a lot of people back home. You think I'm joking or being flip, but I am dead serious. How many cookbooks I've read, stories published, people I've talked to, that raise the roux to some sort of great, mystical thing. They need to get over it. It's a fat and a carbohydrate, not some sort of ethereal transmitter to talk to your long gone, great Cajun grandmother. It is, however, an important component of south Louisiana cuisine.

basic roux

1 cup lipid of choice (i.e. olive oil, bacon grease, duck fat, butter, vegetable oil)
1 cup all-purpose flour

1. Over medium heat, mix the ingredients together and slowly stir until they reach the appropriate color.

There are three basic roux:

1. White, which is good for white gravies and béchamels.
2. Brown, which is the color of a penny, and a good general-purpose roux.
3. Dark, which is good for dishes requiring a richer flavor and a dark color.

The longer you stir, the darker the roux will get, but don't spend more than 1 hour on any roux; it just means your fire is too low and you are wasting your time. I use a heavy cast-iron skillet and a French whisk. Use what works for you. There are no hard-and-fast rules, except one: Burn or scorch it and you have to start over. A burned roux will be bitter and ruin anything you cook with it. You can make roux ahead and store it in an airtight container for up to 1 month in the refrigerator.

When to use: Gumbos, sauces, gravies, alligator sauce piquant, soups

How to make it: Cook slowly over a medium heat in a heavy cast-iron pan. Stir with a whisk or a roux paddle.

How much to use: For gumbos, about 1-inch deep in the bottom of the pot

Backwards roux (roux derriere): A fully cooked roux added at the end of cooking to thicken. Cook an additional 5 minutes after it is added.

Butter, Duck Fat, Olive Oil (the three lipids)

Lipids can be used both as a way to uniformly cook food to preserve it. Typical examples include duck confit, wh is slow-cooked duck submerged in duck fat, and New Or leans BBQ shrimp, which is fast-cooked shrimp submerg in butter. Mix olive oil and butter together to increase the smoking point and add a nice flavor component to sauté foods. Whisk butter, 1 teaspoon at a time, in with a sauce soup or gravy at the end of cooking to add flavor. Remem to adjust your seasonings if you use salted butter.

Flour

Aside from a roux, flour can be mixed with cold water to form a slurry, which is often added to a simmering or bo soup, sauce or gravy. A slurry should be the consistency thick but easily pourable cream. Pour a cold flour slurry slowly into a dish and whisk rapidly to prevent lumps. full thickening power will be achieved when it comes ba up to a simmer. Flour has a flavor component that requir extra minute of cooking after its addition. Otherwise, the sauce, soup or gravy will have an unpleasant "green" fla

Cornstarch

Like flour, when combined with cold water, cornstarch c be used to make a thick but pourable slurry. Execute the same as the flour slurry. Cornstarch is a stronger thickeni agent, so less is needed to achieve the same result. Cornstarch slurry is a neutral flavor component and does not quire extra cooking time, but it still needs to be brought b up to a simmer to achieve its maximum thickening poten

Roux Pâte or Paste

For this technique, mix flour with slightly softened butter. equal parts of flour and butter together and form into pecan size balls. Use right away or cover and refrigerate for later u This roux is whisked into sauces, gravies or soups. Drop th paste in, 1 ball at a time, whisk and check consistency. Use sparingly, remembering that the paste will not reach its full thickening power until the dish comes back up to a simme you miss the mark on a recipe and the result is too thin, use this method to thicken and save the dish. This also adds fla As with a flour slurry, the dish must be cooked for 1 extra minute to finish, to avoid an unpleasant flavor.

BAIN-MARIE

A bain-marie, or "Mary's bath," is simply a pot filled abo halfway with water with a larger stainless-steel bowl plac on top. Bringing the water to a low boil gives a gentler he off of a direct flame. It is most often used to melt chocola or to make delicate sauces.

STOCKS AND BONES

You can make your own homemade stock and freeze it in small plastic zipper-lock bags or ice cube trays. When I peel shrimp or debone a duck, I always save what's left over and make a stock. It is a perfect example of wasting nothing; everything is utilized to maximize flavor.

stock facile (easy stock)

Bones from a chicken, cow, duck, pig and/or turkey, (any combination)
2 sprigs fresh thyme
1 sprig fresh parsley
1 bay leaf
1 tablespoon salt
1 teaspoon black peppercorns
1 onion, halved
1 carrot, roughly chopped
1 stalk celery, roughly chopped
1 toe garlic, crushed
2 gallons water

1. Place the first 10 stock ingredients in a stockpot and cover with water. 2. Bring the fluid to a simmer and cook until the fluid is reduced by half. 3. Strain the ingredients and refrigerate or freeze the stock.

(makes about 1 gallon)

 brown stock

5 pounds beef bones
1 cup tomato paste
2 cups Mirepoix (recipe on page 13)
1 cup cabernet sauvignon
4 toes garlic, crushed
1 tablespoon black peppercorns
1 tablespoon dried thyme
2 tablespoons kosher salt
2 bay leaves
1 teaspoon hot sauce
2 gallons water

1. Preheat oven to 400 degrees. 2. Place the bones in a deep ovenproof pan or pot. Roast in the 400-degree oven for 1 hour. 3. Remove the pan from the oven and brush on the tomato paste. Add the mirepoix; roast for 1 hour. 4. Remove the pan from the oven and place on the stove. Turn burner to medium and add the wine. Deglaze by scraping the bottom of the pan. 5. Add the garlic, peppercorns, thyme, salt, bay leaves, hot sauce and water. Bring to a boil. Reduce heat and simmer over medium-low heat for 2 hours, or until the stock is reduced by half. 6. Strain the stock through a colander and let the contents cool. Refrigerate or freeze for later use in soups, gumbos, jambalayas and other sauces such as Espagnole Sauce (recipe on page 17).

(makes 1 gallon)

duck stock

Duck wing tips, neck bone and carcass
2 cups Mirepoix (recipe on page 13)
4 toes garlic, crushed
1 teaspoon black peppercorns
2 bay leaves
2 sprigs fresh thyme
2 gallons water

1. Combine all stock ingredients in a large stockpot and bring to a boil. 2. Reduce heat to medium-low and simmer for 2 hours or until the stock is reduced to half the original volume. Let the stock cool. 3. Strain through a colander and refrigerate stock. Use within 2 days or freeze and use within 1 month. This stock is perfect for jambalayas, rice, gumbo or in beans in place of water.

(makes 1 gallon)

shrimp stock

10 cups raw shrimp shells *
2 cups Mirepoix (recipe on page 13)
1 teaspoon dried thyme
1 tablespoon salt
1 bay leaf
1 teaspoon hot sauce
1 toe garlic, crushed
1 teaspoon black peppercorns
1 gallon water

1. Place all stock ingredients in a large stockpot. Bring to a boil. 2. Reduce the heat and let the contents simmer for 30 minutes. 3. Remove from heat and let cool. 4. Skim any fat from the top, strain and store the stock in a clean container. Refrigerate and use within 2 days, or freeze it for use within 1 month.

(makes about 1 gallon)

* *When peeling shrimp for other recipes, save the shells and freeze in plastic zipper-lock bags until you have enough to make the stock. Use in any seafood gumbo in place of water.*

Defatting stocks:

Stove method: Place the stockpot on the edge of the burner so that only the edge of the pot is over heat. As the stock comes to a boil, the heat convection will push any floating grease to the opposite and cooler side of the pot. Use a ladle to skim the grease from that side.

Refrigerator method: Place the stock in the refrigerator overnight. Any fat will rise to the surface and solidify. The next day, using a spatula, gently lift off the layer of fat.

SAUCES AND DRESSINGS

hollandaise

4 egg yolks
1 cup butter
Pinch kosher salt
Pinch white pepper
Dash hot sauce
½ lemon, seeded and juiced

1. In a food processor, whisk the egg yolks by pulsing briefly. **2.** In a saucepan, melt the butter until it is very hot but not brown. **3.** With the food processor running, slowly pour the melted butter over the eggs. **4.** Add the salt, pepper, hot sauce and lemon juice. Serve immediately.

(makes 1½ cups)

mayonnaise

2 egg yolks
1 teaspoon Creole mustard
1 teaspoon kosher salt
½ teaspoon white pepper
½ teaspoon garlic powder
1 teaspoon hot sauce
1 tablespoon lemon juice
2 tablespoons water
1½ cups vegetable oil

1. In the top of a bain-marie, whisk all of the mayonnaise ingredients, except the vegetable oil, until the mixture reaches 160 degrees on an instant-read thermometer. (This process along with the lemon juice and heat will help kill any harmful bacteria.) **2.** Remove the bowl from the heat and place contents in a food processor. With the processor running, very slowly add the oil. **3.** Refrigerate immediately in a covered, clean container.

(makes 1½ cups)

crawfish sauce a la thibodaux

This is an easy sauce that works with any type of seafood but is used most commonly with boiled crawfish.

1½ cups fresh Mayonnaise (recipe above)
1 cup ketchup
1 tablespoon hot sauce

1. In a mixing bowl or food processor, combine ingredients and refrigerate until use.

(makes 2½ cups)

remoulade

This sauce works with any type of seafood or seafood salad

1½ cups fresh Mayonnaise (recipe above)
1 cup ketchup
1 tablespoon capers
1 tablespoon salt
1 tablespoon black pepper
1 teaspoon cayenne
1 teaspoon paprika
1 egg, hard-boiled and chopped
½ cup chopped fresh parsley

1. In a mixing bowl or food processor, combine ingredients and refrigerate until use.

(makes 3½ cups)

lié (simple sauce)

- ps beef stock
- blespoon cabernet sauvignon
- easpoon kosher salt
- easpoon black pepper
- easpoon garlic powder
- blespoons cornstarch slurry
- blespoon butter

1 a large stockpot, bring the stock to a boil. **2.** Add the e, salt, pepper and garlic powder. **3.** Add the slurry, 1 ta- spoon at a time, and whisk rapidly until the sauce is thick- d. **4.** To finish, remove the pot from the heat and add er. Adjust the seasonings if needed and serve immediately.

(kes about 2 cups)

shreadeaux

- p butter
- p grated Parmesan cheese
- p grated Asiago cheese
- ps heavy cream
- ch white pepper
- h hot sauce
- ch allspice
- ch cayenne
- ch granulated garlic

1 a medium saucepan, melt the butter. **2.** Over medium t, add the cheeses and stir. **3.** Add the heavy cream, pepper, sauce, allspice, cayenne and garlic. Heat slowly until the ese is melted. **4.** Toss with pasta and serve immediately.

(kes about 5 cups)

pagnole sauce

o called Spanish sauce, this condiment is made with a wn stock, mirepoix, tomato paste and a dark roux. It is basis for other sauces, such as demiglace.

- ps Mirepoix (recipe on page 13)
- p tan roux
- blespoons tomato paste
- allon Brown Stock (recipe on page 15), heated
- es garlic, crushed
- ack peppercorns
- rig fresh thyme
- y leaf

1 a medium sauté pan over medium heat, brown the mire- x in the roux for 5 minutes. **2.** Add the tomato paste and tinue to cook for 5 minutes. **3.** Whisk the hot brown stock vith the mirepoix. Add the garlic, peppercorns, thyme and leaf; simmer over low heat for 1 hour. **4.** Strain and refrig- e the sauce.

(kes ¾ gallon)

marchand de vin sauce (the wine merchant's sauce)

- 6 tablespoons butter
- ½ cup Brown Stock (recipe on page 15)
- ¼ cup diced Tasso (recipe on page 31)
- 1 cup diced mushrooms
- ¼ cup chopped green onion
- 1 toe garlic, minced
- Pinch kosher salt
- 1 cup cabernet sauvignon
- ½ cup Espagnole Sauce (recipe above)

1. In a medium saucepan, melt 4 tablespoons butter. **2.** Add the stock, tasso, mushrooms, green onion, garlic and salt; cook for 3 minutes. **3.** Add the wine and cook for 1 minute. **4.** Add the espagnole sauce and bring to a boil. Reduce the heat to low and allow the mixture to simmer for 15 minutes. **5.** Finish by removing the pan from the heat and adding 2 ta- blespoons of butter.

(makes about 1 ½ cups)

béchamel

- 4 tablespoons salted butter
- Pinch granulated garlic
- Pinch white pepper
- 2 tablespoons flour
- 2 cups milk
- Dash Tabasco sauce

1. In a medium saucepan over low heat, melt the butter. **2.** Add the garlic and pepper. Slowly add the flour and cook for 1 minute, whisking constantly. **3.** Slowly add the milk, whisking constantly. Cook until the sauce is thick, about 1 minute. **4.** Add the Tabasco sauce and serve immediately.

(makes about 2 cups)

bordelaise a la nouvelle orleans

- 4 tablespoons extra-virgin olive oil
- 4 tablespoons butter
- 3 toes garlic, minced
- 2 tablespoons diced green onion
- 2 tablespoons chopped fresh parsley
- 1 teaspoon red wine vinegar
- Pinch kosher salt
- Pinch black pepper

1. In a cold medium saucepan over medium heat, cook the oil, butter and the garlic until the garlic just begins to turn brown. **2.** Add green onion and just heat through. **3.** Add parsley, vinegar, salt and black pepper and serve.

(makes about ½ cup)

béarnaise rouge (red béarnaise)

¼ cup minced red onion
Black pepper, to taste
1 tablespoon tarragon
2 cups cabernet sauvignon *
6 egg yolks
½ cup butter
Juice of ½ lemon

1. In a small sauté pan, place the onion, a pinch of black pepper, ½ tablespoon tarragon and the wine. Bring up to a simmer and allow the mixture to reduce to half the original volume. **2.** Place the egg yolks in a food processor and run very briefly. **3.** In a separate saucepan, melt the butter until it's very hot but not brown. **4.** With the food processor running, slowly pour the hot, melted butter over the egg yolks. **5.** Turn the processor off and add the reduced onion/wine mixture; process for another 30 seconds. **6.** Add the lemon juice and remaining tarragon. Serve immediately with beef or venison.

(makes 2 cups)

* *Substitute a chardonnay for the cabernet to make a White Béarnaise to pair with fish or chicken.*

meuniere

8 tablespoons salted butter
Pinch black pepper
Pinch granulated garlic
2 tablespoons flour
1 cup Shrimp Stock (recipe on page 15) or fish stock
1 teaspoon Worcestershire sauce
1 tablespoon lemon juice
Dash hot sauce

1. In a medium saucepan over medium heat, melt the butter. **2.** Add the pepper and garlic and cook for 30 seconds. **3.** Add the flour and cook for 30 seconds, stirring continuously. **4.** Whisk in the shrimp stock and Worcestershire sauce. Allow the mixture to reduce slightly and the sauce to thicken. **5.** Add the lemon juice and hot sauce and serve immediately.

(makes about 1 cup)

THE SAUTÉ

The sauté, or "jump", is one of the easiest techniques to ter. It's an important one to add to your repertoire.

* Use a clean, large sauté pan.
* Use the minimum amount of oil needed. We are not d frying the food.
* Get the pan hot and the oil very lightly smoking.
* Add the seasoning to the oil.
* Allow enough room to let the food sauté; do not overcrowd the pan or you will be boiling and steaming the fo
* Do not fuss with the pan; allow the food to sauté. Let i and only turn it once.
* Do not sauté shrimp in cast iron, as the shrimp will tu an unappetizing shade of brown.

zydeco's shrimp sauté

1½ pounds fresh gulf shrimp, heads on, or raw, unpeeled 26-30-count tiger shrimp
2 tablespoons extra-virgin olive oil
2 teaspoons kosher salt
2 teaspoons black pepper
1 teaspoon granulated garlic
1 tablespoon thyme leaves
2 tablespoons Worcestershire sauce
1 teaspoon paprika
1 teaspoon hot sauce
¼ teaspoon crab boil seasoning
1 bay leaf
1 lemon, halved
2 tablespoons butter
4 tablespoons chopped fresh parsley
Angel-hair pasta or mirliton, cooked, to serve

1. Peel the shrimp. (Save the shells to make a shrimp sto at a later time.) Get everything together, your "mis en pla **2.** In a large, hot sauté pan, warm the oil. When it just be to smoke, add the salt, pepper, garlic, thyme, Worcesters sauce, paprika, hot sauce, crab boil and bay leaf. Squeeze and drop half of the lemon into the pan. **3.** Add the peele shrimp and stir once. (Do not overcrowd the pan. Make t smaller batches if your pan isn't large enough to accomm date all of the shrimp.) **4.** Sauté the mixture for 3 minute reduce the heat if the pan begins to smoke too heavily or shrimp begin to burn, but do not fuss with the shrimp. **5.** Gently turn the shrimp over and sauté 30 more second until the shrimp are completely pink. Do not overcook th shrimp. **6.** Finish by adding the butter. **7.** Spoon the mixt onto a plate and squeeze the remaining lemon over the shrimp. Adjust seasonings, if needed. Top with freshly chopped parsley and serve with angel-hair pasta or mirli

(serves 4-6)

LOUISIANA FOOD MATRIX

These are a few items used often in south Louisiana cuisine. Use this as a starting point for your recipes.

Alligator
Cooking techniques: poach, braise, fry, grill
Typical dishes: alligator sauce piquant, fried tail meat, grilled alligator ribs
Sauces: crawfish, remoulade, cocktail, meuniere
Typical seasonings/flavorings: thyme, marjoram, basil, oregano, paprika, parsley, garlic, lemon, orange, lime
Pairs well with: pork tasso, Creole tomatoes, mirliton, eggplant, rice, black olives

Crawfish
Cooking techniques: bake, boil, sauté, fry
Typical dishes: crawfish boil, crawfish po'boys, crawfish pie, crawfish alphreadeaux pasta
Sauces: butter, meuniere, crawfish, remoulade, cocktail, mayonnaise
Typical seasonings/flavorings: thyme, New Orleans-style crab boil, paprika, parsley, garlic, lemon, orange, lime
Pairs well with: Creole tomatoes, mirliton, eggplant, potatoes, corn, eggs, pasta, cheese

Crab
Cooking techniques: bake, boil, sauté, fry
Typical dishes: crab boil, crab cakes, salpicon, fried soft-shell crab
Sauces: butter, crawfish, remoulade, cocktail, mayonnaise
Typical seasonings/flavorings: thyme, New Orleans-style crab boil, paprika, parsley, garlic, lemon, orange, lime
Pairs well with: Creole tomatoes, mirliton, mushrooms, spinach, corn, eggs, pasta, cheese

Shrimp
Cooking techniques: sauté, fry, grill
Typical dishes: BBQ, shrimp Creole, shrimp stuffed eggplant, shrimp and mirliton soup, shrimp and andouille sauté
Sauces: butter, crawfish, remoulade, meuniere
Typical seasonings/flavorings: thyme, sage, paprika, cilantro, parsley, garlic, lemon, orange, lime
Pairs well with: pork tasso, Creole tomatoes, mirliton, eggplant, pasta, grits

Catfish, Snapper
Cooking techniques: fry, poach, blacken
Typical dishes: courtbouillion, pecandine
Sauces: butter, bordelaise, meuniere, hollandaise, remoulade, crawfish, aioli
Typical seasonings/flavorings: thyme, basil, marjoram, paprika, garlic, lemon, orange, lime
Pairs well with: pecans, Creole tomatoes, grilled asparagus

Oysters
Cooking techniques: fry, poach, sauté, broil
Typical dishes: raw, red velvet, seafood gumbo, oyster soup
Sauces: butter, meuniere, béchamel, hot, bordelaise
Typical seasonings/flavorings: thyme, paprika, garlic, lemon, orange, lime, horseradish
Pairs well with: french fries, artichoke, spinach, Creole tomatoes, steak au poivre, panéed meats.

Beef
Cooking techniques: blacken, fry, grill, braise
Typical dishes: steak au poivre, panéed meats
Sauces: butter, rouge, marchand de vin, demiglace, bordelaise
Typical seasonings/flavorings: thyme, cumin, coriander, paprika, parsley, garlic, horseradish, tasso
Pairs well with: oysters, Creole tomatoes, potatoes, corn, beets, asparagus, carrots

Poultry, Duck
Cooking techniques: blacken, grill, sauté, confit, poach, braise
Typical dishes: jambalaya, gumbo, duck confit, braised duck with turnips
Sauces: butter, béarnaise blanc, marchand de vin, bordelaise
Typical seasonings/flavorings: thyme, rosemary, cumin, coriander, paprika, parsley, garlic, horseradish, tasso
Pairs well with: oysters, Creole tomatoes, potatoes, corn, beets, asparagus, carrots, turnips, jambalaya, kumquat

Pork
Cooking techniques: blacken, grill, smoke, fry
Typical dishes: cochon, pork tasso, panéed meats, grilliads and grits
Sauces: butter, béarnaise, marchand de vin, demiglace, bordelaise
Typical seasonings/flavorings: thyme, sage, cumin, coriander, paprika, parsley, garlic, horseradish, tasso
Pairs well with: Creole tomatoes, potatoes, corn, beets, asparagus, carrots, apple, kumquat, grits

If you were here in the kitchen right now, watching me type this on a ten-year-old Pismo laptop, you would hear the food truck coming up the back alley, so I have to stop now and put the order away because my employees are late. As I stock the kitchen for the week, go ahead and start a gumbo, make a roux, sauté some shrimp. There are no metal clipboards, no earnest state employees. None of my employees, either. It's just you and me with no real agenda other than to make great food. When I get done with the order, we can start with the softshell crabs in the sink. They are cruising around in a bowl of Mooresville's finest tap water like they're riding on an aquatic merry-go-round.

chapter

With all the great game, seafood, chicken, alligator, pork and beef hanging around, and various settlers with their various recipes, things in New Orleans were bound to get tasty.

IS THAT ANDOUILLE
IN YOUR POCKET OR ARE YOU HAPPY TO SEE ME?
(29.88210, -90.39710)

Nothing says more about Louisiana cuisine than its local sausages and seasoning meats. With all the great game, seafood, chicken, alligator, pork and beef hanging around, plus the French, German, Spanish, Italian and Hungarian settlers all over the place, and those settlers getting together and comparing recipes, and all those people getting together and making shiny new, itsy bitsy baby people and all that fun, new recipes develop. It's then you really start to get cooking.

A case in point: My formative years were spent in Les Côte Des Allemands (the German Coast), an area named by the French. It was a beautiful, verdant area of land on the eastern edge of Acadiana. It hugs the Mississippi River, just southwest of and impinging New Orleans. It was fortuitous the area was named the German Coast, because it just so happened that a ton of German immigrants got together and set up residence there, including some of my not-so-distant ancestors.

As it turns out, they were ecstatic about getting out of their dumpy old flats in Europe and hanging out in their new digs with the local French population of Louisiana. Knowing a good thing when they saw it, the Germans Frenchified their last names, lost their umlauts and bilabial fricatives and started parling the much sexier langue française. Of course, one thing led to another and a few generations later, the resulting progeny got together and, by unanimous vote, fixed the damned andouille.

Louisiana andouille is not the andouille of France, which is made with milk, intestines and other whacky stuff. This is a big man's Louisiana sausage, made with big meats from the German Coast. It's the perfect recipe for me because it's an excuse to buy exotic culinary equipment like machines with knobs and switches and shiny, sharp spinning blades and, of course, big hunks of pork. One gets the added bonus of making the obvious rude and inappropriate jokes during the stuffing process and at the end, we all get to play with fire and smoke! What could be better?

That's how all Louisiana sausages and seasoning meats were developed, as a result of all of that indigenous debauchery, creativity and enticing fires of all types so many years ago. And it goes into some of the most famous south Louisiana dishes: red beans and rice, duck and andouille jambalaya, chicken and sausage gumbo, chaurice and eggs, saucisse cocodrie with potatoes. Here then are some of the sausage and seasoning meat recipes that are made every day back in south Louisiana and that I make and use on a regular basis at Zydeco's 5.

Retrigerate these sausages immediately or freeze the andouille in plastic freezer storage bags.

andouille
(ahn-DOO-ee)

Good andouille is easy to make with a few well-chosen, fresh, local ingredients. If I had a logo, coat of arms, avatar or shield, it would include a big, rude, angry link of heavily smoked andouille. This is the sausage that made Louisiana famous and I was fortunate enough to live in Les Côte Des Allemands, where amazing andouille was everywhere. * I have an old recipe that uses hand-cut pork, salt, black pepper, fresh garlic and cayenne. It is smoked for long hours over sugarcane and pecan wood until it turns almost black. The old, smoky fumoirs that dotted the German Coast would crank out miles and miles of the stuff every year. Most of those old smokehouses are gone, but you can get a pretty good commercially produced andouille at the Louisiana supermarkets. It's a bit harder to find really good andouille anywhere else, though the Internet helps. * This recipe is one that I have successfully used over the years at The Z and continue to tweak. It has a complex flavor – sweet, savory, piquant, earthy – and makes a great accompaniment to white beans and rice.

makes 4 pounds

- ½ cup chopped garlic
- 1 tablespoon cayenne pepper
- ½ tablespoon dried thyme
- 2 tablespoons paprika
- ½ cup chopped fresh parsley
- ¼ cup brown sugar
- 1 tablespoon red pepper flakes
- 1 teaspoon fast cure *
- 5 tablespoons kosher salt
- ¼ cup cracked black pepper
- 5 pounds pork shoulder
- ½ pound pork fat

1. Preheat a smoker. **2.** In a medium bowl, mix together all of the spices and seasonings (garlic, cayenne pepper, thyme, paprika, parsley, brown sugar, red pepper flakes, fast cure, salt and pepper). Set aside. **3.** Cut the pork shoulder into ¼-inch dice. Chop the fat very fine. Place the cut pork and fat into a large bowl. **4.** Add the seasonings to the meat and fat and mix well. **5.** Carefully stuff the seasoned meat mixture into the meat casing, making 12-inch-long links. (For more on making links, see Tricks of the Trade, page 27.) **6.** Place the andouille links in the smoker and cook until the internal temperature of the sausage reaches 165 degrees.

*Fast cures like Prague Powder No 1 Pink Curing Salt, used to kill harmful bacteria, are available at most butcher shops, online, at Zydeco's 5 or on our Web site, zydecos.net

Refrigerate the links and use within 3 days or freeze for up to 1 month. To serve, steam, broil or grill the boudin, or poach them in beer.

boudin
(BOO-dan)
THE SAUSAGE OF LAFAYETTE

The pan sits next to the register, steam swirling up, out and down from the lip. The smell of pork piggybacks on the steam and fills my nose. * I ask for, "One, no make it two," and the woman behind the counter walks over to the sputtering pan, lifts the dented metal lid and removes one silver cylinder, then another. The foil-wrapped packages are swiftly dropped into a brown paper bag. She gives it to me with a handful of paper towels and packets of Creole mustard. * In that pan sits row upon row of boudin blanc, or just boudin for short. They're plump sausages of pork, rice and vegetables, encased in a rubbery, chewy skin. The boudin have probably been sitting there steaming since early that morning, wrapped up like mummies, getting better with each passing minute. Boudin was created out of necessity and is still made today out of love. The vegetables and rice were added to extend the sausage in times when pork was scarce. As is often the case, recipes from necessity can make great food. * Louisiana boudin has transformed into a nomadic sausage, greedily gobbled up by busy south Louisiana travelers, like fast food in a tube. The capitol of Cajun country, Lafayette, has some of the best boudin, though there is a greasy little place in Boutte with some amazing links. It's found in almost every gas station from Lake Charles to New Orleans, and is great poached in Abita beer or seared in a cast-iron skillet and dipped in Creole mustard. * There are different ways to eat boudin. One can devour the sausage, biting through the chewy casing, or one can peel the boudin out of its cocoon, unceremoniously bite off the end of the sausage and suck out the contents. A gentle squeeze facilitates the process and is easier when driving down Highway 90, I-10 or LA 1. * This recipe is broken up into three main components: the liver, the pork and the rice.

liver

1 pound pork liver
8 cups cool, fresh water

1. Rinse the pork liver and drain. **2.** Place the liver in a stockpot and add the water, covering the liver completely. **3.** Cover the pot with a lid and place on the stovetop over medium heat. Bring the liver to a low boil. Cook for 10 minutes. **4.** Remove the pot from the heat and discard the liquid. Set aside to cool.

(recipe continued on page 26)

(recipe continued from page 25)

pork and rice

- 5 pounds pork butt, cut into 2-inch cubes
- 1 bay leaf
- 4 cups diced onions
- 4 cups diced red, yellow and/or green bell peppers
- 1 cup diced celery
- 2 tablespoons fresh thyme leaves
- 2 tablespoons whole black peppercorns
- 2 teaspoons cayenne powder
- 6 tablespoons salt
- 2 cups rice
- 4 cups reserved pork broth
- 6 cups pork stock
- 2 cups chopped green onions
- 2 cups chopped fresh parsley

1. Place the cubed pork, bay leaf, onions, bell peppers, celery, thyme, perppercorns, cayenne and salt in a large stockpot. 2. Cover the meat with water and place the pot on the stovetop over medium-high heat. Bring the mixture to a boil. Reduce the heat to low and allow the meat to simmer for 30 minutes, or until cooked through. 3. Drain the pork; reserve the pork broth in one container and the vegetables in another container. Discard the bay leaf and set aside to cool. 4. Place the rice and pork broth in a small stockpot. Cook the rice over high heat until it reaches a boil. Reduce the heat to medium-low and cook for 30 minutes, or until tender. Remove the pot from the heat and use a fork to fluff the rice; cool. 5. To assemble, set up your sausage machine with a coarse die and grind the cooked pork, liver and reserved vegetables. 6. To a large bowl, add all of the ground pork ingredients and the cooked rice. Add 6 cups of pork stock, the green onions and the parsley. Mix gently and adjust the salt, pepper and/or cayenne pepper, if needed. 7 Stuff the mixture into clean pork casings, making 12-inch-long links. (For more on making links, see Tricks of the Trade, page 27.)

How to eat boudin blanc

1. Fill up your car with gas. Clean it well, inside and out. 2. Fill up your MP3 player with BeauSoleil and Wayne Toups. 3. Get a bunch of your friends together. 4. Steam up a big batch of boudin. 5. Wrap the links in aluminum foil. 6. Place the hot boudin in an insulated container (such as a Styrofoam ice chest). 7. Fill a squeeze bottle, just one, full of Creole mustard. 8. Acquire a roll of paper towels. 9. Get into the car with the friends, the boudin, the mustard and the paper towels. 10. Drive down the closest scenic highway or even just around the block with the tunes cranked up and the windows rolled down. Pass around the boudin and the mustard and enjoy, knowing there are thousands of people in south Louisiana doing exactly the same thing at that very moment.

* If you do not have a sausage machine, you can get good results by cutting the meats by hand or using a food processor. The texture will be different, but the flavor will be the same.

makes 6 pounds

chaurice (shah-REES)

This is a spicy New Orleans sausage with a strong Spanish heritage. Louisiana was, for a time, a part of Spain, and New Orleans was its capitol. This is when Louisiana chaurice made its debut. Chaurice is a not-so-dissimilar variation of Spanish chorizo, and is traditionally served for breakfast, sautéed with potatoes or Creole eggs. It wouldn't be out of character for chaurice to show up on a jazz brunch menu back home, either, which is why I routinely feature it on ours.

chaurice

- ½ cup minced garlic
- ¼ cup minced onion
- ¼ cup minced bell pepper
- 2 tablespoons cayenne pepper
- 4 tablespoons paprika
- 3 tablespoons kosher salt
- 2 tablespoons red pepper flakes
- 1 teaspoon fresh thyme
- 1 teaspoon cumin
- 1 teaspoon allspice
- 1 teaspoon dried oregano
- ½ teaspoon ground bay leaf
- 1 teaspoon fast cure
- 5 pounds pork shoulder

1. Preheat a smoker. 2. In a large mixing bowl, combine all of the vegetables and seasonings. Set aside. 3. Run the pork through a sausage machine with a coarse die. 4. Add the ground meat to the bowl with the seasonings and mix well. 5. Stuff the mixture into meat casings, making 12-inch-long links. (For more on making links, see Tricks of the Trade, right.) 6. Place the chaurice links into the smoker and cook until the internal temperature of the sausage reaches 165 degrees.

tricks of the trade

1. In sausage making, cleanliness and temperature control are very important. Make sure that all of your equipment is clean. Make sure that your work area is clean. Wear latex gloves. Clean all of the equipment and the work area thoroughly after you have finished. Disinfect work surfaces with a mild solution of bleach and water.
2. Make sure that the meat is very cold. When I make andouille, the meat is right at 33 degrees and just slightly frozen. It makes it easier to cut and keeps nasty little bacteria from making an unwelcome appearance. I have a pan with a layer of ice cubes in it next to the sausage machine. As I make the links, I place them in the ice to keep them as cold as possible. Rinse the finished sausages under cold water to remove any particles, then promptly refrigerate, cook or freeze the sausage.
3. If you don't want to use casing for your sausages, you can simply wrap the processed meat very tightly in plastic wrap, refrigerate it overnight, remove the plastic wrap and smoke or cook the next day. The sausages can also be formed into patties, wrapped and smoked, cooked and refrigerated or frozen as needed.
4. Making sausage links takes a bit of practice. Load the sausage machine tube with the cleaned and rinsed casing. Tie the end of the casing. When the sausage is at the correct length, gently turn the sausage link three times toward you. Continue with the next link but do not twist that one. Pinch where the link will be and continue to the third link. At the end of the third link, twist three times toward you. Continue this process of pinching and twisting alternate links.
5. Run a slice or two of fresh bread through the machine at the end to push out the remaining meat. As the bread just begins to come through the nozzle, turn off the machine and tie off the last sausage.
6. Pork casings, which can be found at your local butcher shop or online, are heavily salted and need to be rinsed with cold water inside and out. Allow the casings to soak for 30 minutes. I place a bowl of rinsed casings in the sink and allow a small stream of cold water to run over them to remove any trace of salt.

makes 4 pounds

To serve, steam, smoke, boil or grill the links to an internal temperature of 165 degrees.

boutte alligator sausage
(SAUCISSE COCODRIE A LA BOUTTE)

Boutte, Louisiana, is the home of the annual Boutte Alligator Festival. Since I went to high school there, it's also a very special little town to me. The festival is a chance to dance the Zydeco with the pretty young ladies at the Fais Do Do and to eat rich, savory foods and pay homage to Le Cocodrie (the Louisiana gator). Large and amazing alligator po'boys are a big favorite down there, as well as fried alligator tail and of course the famous alligator sauce piquant, a spicy mixture of Creole tomatoes, black olives and gator meat. Here is my recipe for an exceptional alligator sausage that you would be proud to serve at your next Boutte fête.

makes 6 pounds

- 3 tablespoons kosher salt
- 1 tablespoon coarse-ground black pepper
- 1 teaspoon ground allspice
- 1 teaspoon cayenne pepper
- 1 teaspoon fast cure *
- 1 quart buttermilk (optional) †
- 5 pounds alligator tail meat **
- ½ pound pork shoulder ††
- ½ pound pork fat ††

1. In a medium mixing bowl, combine all of the seasonings. Set aside. 2. Pick through the alligator meat, removing and discarding any excess fat, tendons or foreign matter. Rinse the meat under cool, fresh water. Drain the meat and pat dry with paper towels. 3. Cut the alligator, pork and pork fat into cubes and run it through a sausage machine with a coarse die. 4. Combine the meats, fat and seasonings and mix well. 5. Stuff the mixture into pork middle casings, making 9-inch-long links. (For more on making links, see Tricks of the Trade, page 27.) 6. Rinse the links under cool water to remove any foreign particles. Refrigerate or freeze immediately in plastic freezer storage bags. Cook within 3 days or freeze for up to 1 month.

* Fast cures like Prague Powder No. 1 Pink Curing Salt, used to kill harmful bacteria, are available at most butcher shops, online, at Zydeco's 5 or on our Web site, zydecos.net.

† For a milder flavor, soak the alligator in buttermilk overnight in the refrigerator. Drain and rinse well the next day. Proceed with the recipe as normal.

** You can find alligator tail meat at most seafood purveyors, at Zydeco's 5 or on our Web site, zydecos.net.

†† The addition of pork and pork fat is important to this recipe. The sausage will be too lean and dry without it.

Cool and refrigerate the cooked tasso until needed

tasso

How cool is it that we use meat as a seasoning? Tasso is a spicy jerky made from all of the leftover bits of a butchered pig, and is typically used to jazz up the local dishes. Today, people are tassoing everything, including fish, beef and chicken. This is a simple little recipe I use at Zydeco's incorporating pork tenderloin, but the recipe will work equally well with less-expensive cuts of meat.

tasso seasoning

- 1 cup coarse-ground black pepper
- 1 cup kosher salt
- 1 cup cayenne powder
- 1 cup brown sugar
- 1½ cups granulated garlic
- 1 tablespoon allspice

1. Combine all tasso seasoning ingredients and set aside.

tasso

- 1 5-pound pork tenderloin, sliced into ¼-inch-thick rounds
- 5 cups Worcestershire sauce
- 5 cups Tasso Seasoning (recipe above)

1. Marinate the sliced pork tenderloin in Worcestershire sauce overnight. **2.** Remove the meat and drain. **3.** Place the tasso seasoning onto a large, flat platter and dredge the pork in the seasoning, coating both sides. **4.** Layer the pork in a large colander, covering each layer with extra seasoning. Place the colander in a large pan to catch any liquids, cover with aluminum foil and refrigerate for at least 3 days. **5.** Preheat a smoker. **6.** Remove the meat and place in the preheated smoker. Cook until the tasso reaches an internal temperature of 155 degrees.

makes **3** pounds

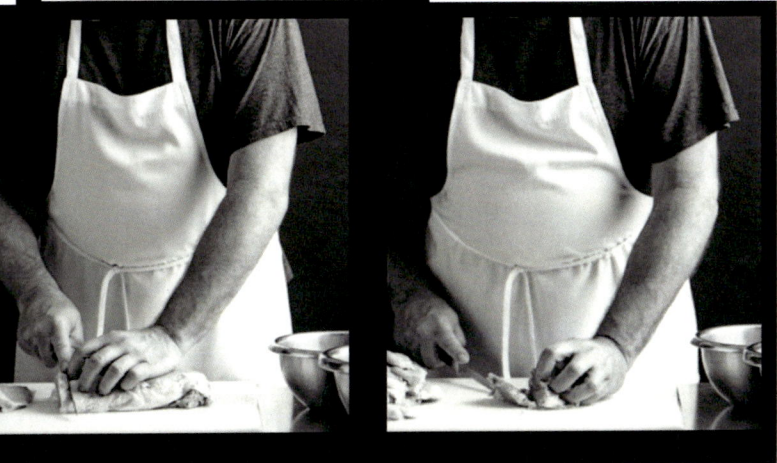

Refrigerate and allow the ingredients to soak for at least 3 days.

pickled meats*
(29.88079, -90.43545)

On the corner, stands Monsieur Oscar's Mercantile, a long, cypress wooden structure, sagging slightly and sporting rows of doors and windows, abutting Lafaille Street, facing Old Spanish Trail. Tattered screens cover the openings, giving some protection against the onslaught of cousins (koo-zans), or mosquitoes, as big as your hand and known to come down and snatch up children from their mother's grasp and small dogs from their master's leash. I don't know why the Cajun language uses the same word for blood-sucking insects as it does your aunt and uncle's kids, but I digress. * Mr. Oscar's, where my cousin Skeeter (yes, his real name) and I walked, coin in pocket, empty bottles in hand, allowed us to buy small bits of preserved and pickled meats for lunch. The empty bottles were returnable, in a time when you brought back empties for a penny each. The thick, faceted glass bottles from Zetz or Barq's would fetch an extra penny, so Skeeter and I were always on the lookout for those. * We would pull back the double screen doors, throw our bottles and money on the counter at Mr. Oscar, run back to the back of the store and work our way up to the front, looking over each and every item for its intrinsic value. Ultimately, we would return to the counter, eying large jars of pickled meats, piquant boiled and brined eggs, wax packets of sun-dried shrimps and other treats. The jars lined up on the counter were bright red crystal, gleaming and containing exotic tasty bits. * Settling on a fair price for our bottles and combining our coins, we would make our purchases and walk out with our bounty, laughing and eating the tart pickled meats in the summer sun. Skeeter has since passed away and Monsieur Oscar's is long gone, but I know that the laughter of two young cousins still echoes in that long, cypress wooden structure, sagging slightly and sporting rows of doors and windows, abutting Lafaille Street, facing Old Spanish Trail. * Today, there is a small and devoted group of people who wouldn't cook a bean without pickled meat and I must admit, I am one of them. I think it's because of all of those trips to Mr. Oscar's. This is a very simple recipe for pickled meat that is used to season any bean dish, including red beans and rice.

- 1 quart white vinegar
- ¼ cup mustard seed
- 1 large sprig fresh thyme
- ½ cup sliced red onion
- 1 whole cayenne pepper
- 1 bay leaf
- 4 toes garlic, sliced
- 2 tablespoons kosher salt
- 2 tablespoons black peppercorns
- 1 3-pound pork shoulder, sliced ½-inch thick and trimmed of excess fat

1. Into a medium pan, place all of the pickled meats ingredients, except the pork. Bring to a simmer and cook for 10 minutes. **2.** Remove the pan from the heat and allow it to cool. **3.** Pour the mixture into a large glass jar. Add the pork, being sure to completely submerge the meat in the liquid.

*Use pickled meats in bean dishes like red beans and rice

Makes 3 pounds

chapter 2

SUNDAY BRUNCH
A BEAUTIFUL AND DIGNIFIED LADY ONCE AGAIN

Sunday brunch is the time for New Orleans to transform into her dignified Creole persona. The lady removes her gaudy apparel, the clothes that would normally entice and lure the less sophisticated among us. The fishnet stockings are put away, cherry red lipstick wiped off, the bustier and beads tucked away. In their place, tasteful silk stockings are carefully pulled up, a beautiful dress is donned and hair is tastefully done. A southern accent mixes with a slight hint of French perfume.

Her once-deadly siren songs, luring unsuspecting tourists to their doom, are now sweet, melodic, comforting jazz riffs. Her table is resplendent with samples of the local bounty: grits, oysters, duck, beef, pork, crawfish, eggs, rabbit, alligator, citrus and more. Drinks are poured, thick coffee and chicory is brewed. The absinthe and mimosas flow.

The transformation is complete and she presents herself to us. The table spans not so much physical space, but that of time and history; a spread straddling more than 200 years of narrative. She is calling us to that table to partake on silver platters and from porcelain cups. The music swirls around us and we are presented with amazing dishes, as we sit on ancient, decorative wrought-iron balconies. The more adult and sophisticated New Orleans, often lost amid her more rambunctious activities, is reborn. She is a beautiful lady once again and for a time, puts aside the serious problems that plague her.

It is during this time Zydeco's transforms herself as well. From the fried bar food, buffalo wings, chicken nuggets, french fries, things covered in cheese and some of the stereotypical, slightly skewed and cliché New Orleans recipes that some demand. She moves away from the whacky Christmas tree lights, the beads, the gallons of big-ass beers and inappropriate show tunes. She moves to what I consider more of the essence of Louisiana. Sunday brunch? Well, that's one beautiful lady.

35

Garnish each omelet with shredded cheese, the remaining tarragon, slices of Creole tomato and green onion.

crawfish, tasso AND CHAURICE OMELET
WITH SHREDDED PEPPER JACK CHEESE

Here is a très bon version of a crawfish omelet that is always on Zydeco's Sunday brunch menu. When I was a young boy, picking the remaining crawfish tail meat for mom after a Saturday boil guaranteed I was going to get a fresh crawfish omelet on Sunday morning. Quite the incentive, and you know I was happy to oblige.

- 1 stick (8 tablespoons) butter
- 1 pound crawfish tail meat
- ½ pound pork Tasso (recipe on page 31), diced
- 1 pound Chaurice sausage (recipe on page 27), diced
- 12 eggs
- 2 tablespoons tarragon leaves
- 1 teaspoon cayenne pepper
- 1 pound shredded hot pepper Monterey Jack cheese
- Kosher salt, to taste
- Black pepper, to taste
- 2 Creole tomatoes *, thinly sliced, to garnish
- ½ cup diced green onion, to garnish

1. In a large sauté pan, lightly brown 4 tablespoons butter. Add the crawfish, tasso and chaurice and sauté over high heat for 1 minute to heat through. 2. Remove the pan from the heat and cover to keep warm. 3. In a large mixing bowl, whisk the eggs. Fold in 1 tablespoon tarragon leaves and the cayenne pepper. 4. Put 1 tablespoon of butter in a hot nonstick sauté pan and allow it to melt and begin to brown. Pour one-fourth of the egg mixture into the pan. Allow the omelet to set for about 1 minute. 5. Using a rubber spatula, flip the omelet over. 6. Add one-fourth of the crawfish mixture and about 2 ounces of cheese and continue to cook for 1 minute, until the omelet is just set. 7. Slide the omelet onto a plate. Season with salt and pepper, to taste. 8. Repeat 3 times to make 4 omelets.

*Creole tomatoes are medium-size tomatoes native to New Orleans. If they don't have them at your farmers market, grab your favorite local variety

serves 4

Top with chopped parsley and serve with pickled mirliton spears and French bread croutons.

oyster + chicken LIVER EN BROCHETTE WITH SWEET MIRLITON SPEARS & NEW ORLEANS BORDELAISE (ANGELS AND DEVILS ON HORSEBACK)

This is a rich, earthy and elegant dish perfect for a Sunday brunch. The gulf oysters and chicken livers are wrapped in bacon and skewered (en brochette), then grilled to perfection in the oyster shells. A New Orleans bordelaise is made from the pan drippings and adds a wonderful high note that complements and balances the earthiness of the dish. The mirliton spears give a sweet finish.

sweet refrigerator mirliton spears

- 1 cup vinegar
- ½ cup sugar
- 1 toe garlic, smashed
- 1 teaspoon salt
- 1 tablespoon mustard seed
- 1 Tabasco pepper
- 1 teaspoon black peppercorns
- 2 mirlitons, peeled, seeded and cut into ½-inch spears

1. Place all of the mirliton spears ingredients into a clean, sterilized canning jar. **2.** Refrigerate for 3 days.

french bread croutons

- 1 loaf day-old French bread
- 1 cup extra-virgin olive oil
- 2 tablespoons kosher salt
- 2 tablespoons coarse-ground black pepper
- 2 tablespoons marjoram
- 2 tablespoons granulated garlic

1. Preheat oven to 350 degrees. **2.** Cut the French bread on the bias, making about 24 1-inch slices. Place the slices in an ovenproof pan. **3.** Drizzle olive oil over the bread. Top the slices with salt, pepper, marjoram and granulated garlic. **4.** Bake in the 350-degree oven for 30 minutes or until the bread is completely dry and light brown. Set aside.

oyster and chicken livers

- 12 large, fresh gulf oysters
- 1½ cups rock salt
- 24 slices (about 2 pounds) thick, hickory-smoked bacon
- 12 chicken livers
- 1 teaspoon paprika
- 1 teaspoon kosher salt
- 1 teaspoon coarse-ground black pepper

1. Preheat oven or broiler to 425 degrees. **2.** Shuck the oysters, saving the shells and reserving the liquor. Rinse the shells and dry with a clean towel. **3.** Place the rock salt in little mounds on the platters, a few tablespoons for each mound, 12 mounds for each platter. Divide the 24 shells evenly between the two platters, pushing the shells gently into the mounds of salt. The rock salt will keep the shells level and steady. Carefully put the platters aside. **4.** In a medium sauté pan over medium heat, fry the bacon until just cooked through and still soft, about 3 minutes on one side, an additional 1 minute on the other side. Do not let the bacon become crisp or burn. If the pan is too hot and the oil is smoking, reduce the heat. Reserve the bacon and cool. Drain the excess bacon grease from the pan and keep the drippings in an airtight container for use another time. **5.** Wrap each of the 12 oysters in one slice of cooked bacon. Use a toothpick on each one to hold the bacon in place. Place the oysters in the prepared shells. **6.** Wrap the 12 chicken livers in the remaining slices of cooked bacon. Use a toothpick on each one to hold the bacon in place. Place the chicken livers in the remaining oyster shells. Transfer all of the shells to a baking sheet. **7.** Lightly season the oysters and livers with paprika, salt and pepper. **8.** Broil the chicken livers for 10-15 minutes, or until they are cooked completely through and the internal temperature reaches 165 degrees on an instant-read digital thermometer. **9.** Broil the oysters for 10-15 minutes or until they reach an internal temperature of 135 degrees on an instant-read digital thermometer. **10.** Transfer the livers and oysters back to the serving platters.

New Orleans bordelaise sauce

- 2 tablespoons butter
- ⅛ cup minced red onion
- 4 toes garlic, sliced
- 1 cup chardonnay
- Oyster liquor (reserved above)
- 2 tablespoons chopped green onion
- 2 tablespoons chopped fresh parsley, plus more to garnish
- ½ lemon
- Sweet Mirliton Spears (recipe above), to serve
- French Bread Croutons (recipe above), to serve

1. To the pan where you fried the bacon over medium heat, add the butter. When the butter melts and begins to lightly brown, add the red onion. Cook for 1 minute. **2.** Add the sliced garlic and cook for 30 seconds. **3.** Add the chardonnay and oyster liquor. Turn the heat up to medium-high and cook for 2 minutes, stirring often. **4.** Reduce the heat to medium. Add the green onion and parsley and cook for 30 seconds. Squeeze in the juice from the lemon. **5.** Remove the pan from the heat. Pour the sauce into a container and keep warm. **6.** Drizzle the finished sauce over the oysters and livers.

serves 6-8

Distribute the onions among 4 plates and top with boudin or arrange the meat on an elegant serving platter.

german coast
BOUDIN WITH ONIONS, BEER AND CREOLE MUSTARD PAN SAUCE

Here, we take southwest Louisiana boudin and apply a German Coast spin by using plenty of onions and a unique, memorable Louisiana beer. The result is a hearty, earthy dish. The Creole mustard pan sauce pairs well with the boudin and lends a smart finish.

- 4 onions
- 4 tablespoons extra-virgin olive oil
- 4 links Boudin (recipe on page 25)
- 1 tablespoon dried thyme leaves
- 2 toes garlic, thinly sliced
- 2 teaspoons kosher salt
- 2 teaspoons black pepper
- ¼ cup balsamic vinegar
- 1 bottle dark Louisiana beer
- 3 tablespoons Creole mustard *

1. Peel and cut the onions lengthwise; cut the halves into paper-thin strips. 2. In a medium saucepan, heat the olive oil until it is lightly smoking. Add the boudin and brown for approximately 5 minutes on each side. Remove and set aside. 3. Add the onions, thyme, garlic, salt and black pepper to the saucepan. Cover the pan and cook the mixture for 10 minutes. Add the vinegar and cook for 5 additional minutes, until most of the vinegar has cooked off. 4. Add the boudin back to the pan and add the beer. Cover and simmer over low heat for 10 minutes. 5. Add the Creole mustard and cook for an additional 1 minute.

serves 2-4

*Try Zatarain's Creole mustard, available at most well-stocked grocery stores, online at zatarains.com, at Zydeco's, or on our Web site, zydecos.net. You can also use coarse-ground mustard.

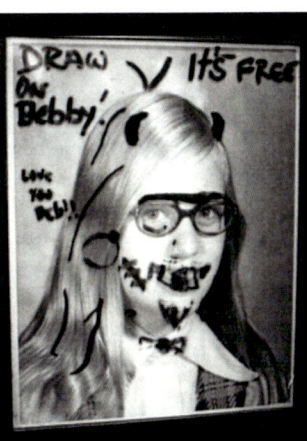

Top with freshly chopped parsley and a slice of lemon

shrimp sauté
WITH FRIED GRIT CAKES AND BÉCHAMEL SAUCE

On the West Bank, a line of dented and battered pickup trucks form a lazy semicircle on an oyster shell parking lot. The sunlight beats through the thick, hot, humid Louisiana air. Is it possible the atmosphere will spontaneously combust or will it just steam you alive? This may be the day we find out. In the truck beds, scales hang down with the weight of galvanized tin pans and scoops. Beneath them, white foam ice chests are in neat rows, on which are scrawled cryptic designations: U10, 16-20, 26-30, 110-130 gumbos, poisson, bustahs. ✶ The oyster shells crunch underfoot as you eye the arc of trucks. The one with the "Go Saints" sign plastered on the side looks promising, so you walk up to the old Ford. An elderly lady is sitting under a tattered umbrella next to the red truck listening to a large black and chrome boom box, dribbling a barely audible country song out into the thick air. The lady smiles as you ask for a few pounds of the 16-20s. ✶ She opens up the appropriate chest and scoops out a matrix of crushed ice and fresh gulf shrimp. You notice that the shrimp have no telltale orange spot along the top edge of their heads. Here is an important fact that not many people know: Shrimp have a built-in temperature gauge. If they are off the ice too long that temperature gauge, a spot on the back of their head, turns bright orange. They belie freshness and should be avoided. Just a little something to remember. These crustaceans, however, are beautiful and fresh, gray-green and harvested that morning. Carefully weighing the shrimp, the kind and gentle lady deftly pours them into a plastic bag, which she places first into a brown paper bag and then finally into a cardboard box. Your small ice chest is in the trunk, waiting to accept the shrimp. ✶ Seafood is a big part of the cuisine along the Gulf Coast. It is plentiful and fresh. The shrimpers' wives, daughters and mothers sell their catch along with fresh fish and softshell crabs. This recipe offers shrimp sautéed in olive oil, thyme and garlic and transformed with the addition of a rich béchamel. The spicy and smooth shrimp are then spooned over fried grit cakes. A wonderful dish indeed.

grit cakes

Butter, as needed
5 cups water
1 tablespoon kosher salt
1 cup quick grits

1. Generously butter the sides of an 8" x 12" rectangular loaf pan and line the bottom with wax paper or plastic wrap. **2.** In a large stockpot, combine the water and salt and bring to a boil. **3.** Slowly whisk in the grits and turn the burner to medium-low. Cover and simmer for 5-7 minutes, stirring often. **4.** When the grits are fully cooked and thick, pour them into the greased pan. Let cool. **5.** Place the grits in the refrigerator overnight. **6.** Remove the grits from the pan and cut into 8 slices.

(recipe continued on page 44)

serves 8

café NOUVELLE ORLEANS

This is my favorite Sunday brunch drink; easy to make and very flavorful.

1 cup New Orleans coffee and chicory
1 shot Chambord

1. Combine the cocktail ingredients in your desired cocktail glass and serve.

(serves 1)

(recipe continued from page 43)

shrimp sauté

½ cup extra-virgin olive oil
2 teaspoons kosher salt
2 teaspoons black pepper
1 teaspoon granulated garlic
1 tablespoon thyme leaves
2 tablespoons Worcestershire sauce
1 teaspoon paprika
1 teaspoon hot sauce
¼ teaspoon crab boil seasoning
1 bay leaf
½ lemon
1½ pounds raw 26-30-count tiger shrimp, peeled and cleaned

1. Into a large, hot sauté pan, pour the olive oil. When it just begins to smoke, add all of the ingredients, except the lemon and shrimp. Cook for 1 minute. **2.** Squeeze the lemon over the mixture and drop it into the pan; stir well to combine. Add the peeled shrimp and stir. Sauté the mixture for 3-4 minutes. Reduce the heat if the pan begins to smoke too heavily or the shrimp begin to burn. Sauté until the shrimp are completely pink and just cooked through, about 3 minutes. (Do not overcook the shrimp.) **3.** Use the pan (and drippings) to start the béchamel sauce (recipe below).

frying

1 cup flour
4 eggs
½ cup water
3 dashes Tabasco sauce
1 cup bread crumbs
1 teaspoon dried thyme leaves
1 teaspoon black pepper
1 teaspoon garlic powder
8 cups vegetable oil

1. Prepare a frying station. Into one shallow dish, place the flour. To a second shallow dish, add the eggs and water. Whisk the water with the eggs until well combined; add the Tabasco. Into a third shallow dish, add the bread crumbs, thyme, black pepper and garlic powder. **2.** Into a 4-quart pot, insert an instant-read thermometer and heat the vegetable oil to 350 degrees. **3.** Dredge the grit cakes first in flour, then the egg mixture, then in the bread crumb mixture. **4.** Fry the breaded cakes, in batches if necessary, for 5 minutes. Remove and place on paper towels to drain. **5.** Distribute the fried grit cakes among 8 warm plates. Using a slotted spoon or tongs, transfer two shrimp to the top of each of the grit cakes.

béchamel sauce

Shrimp Sauté pan drippings
2 tablespoons butter
2 tablespoons flour
2 cups half-and-half
Pinch granulated garlic
2 dashes Tabasco sauce
Pinch salt
½ cup chopped fresh parsley
8 slices lemon

1. Turn the heat to low and add the butter to the pan used for the shrimp sauté. **2.** Whisk the flour into the pan drippings and cook for 1 minute, whisking continuously. **3.** Slowly pour the half-and-half into the pan, then add the granulated garlic and whisk well. Cook for about 1 minute. **4.** When the sauce is thick enough to coat the back of a spoon, add the hot sauce and salt. Cook for 5 minutes. **5.** To serve, spoon the béchamel sauce over the shrimp and grits.

broiled frog legs
WITH CRAB RAVIGOTE, ASPARAGUS AND CREOLE TOMATO

I never thought that frog legs would generate as much interest as they have at The Z. We can't seem to make enough. Taking a slight detour from a somewhat hackneyed fried dinner, these broiled frog legs are paired with a cool and creamy ravigote of lump crabmeat, asparagus and Creole tomato. It makes a wonderful dish for Sunday brunch.

tomatoes

2 Creole tomatoes, sliced *

asparagus

1 pound chilled asparagus
4 tablespoons olive oil
1 teaspoon salt
1 teaspoon black pepper

1. Preheat a grill to medium heat. 2. Cut or snap off about 1 inch of the tough root end of each asparagus spear. 3. In a deep plate or shallow bowl, combine the olive oil, salt and pepper. Roll each piece of asparagus in the oil mixture. 4. Grill the asparagus for 5 minutes, turning occasionally to cook evenly. 5. Remove from the grill and chill in the refrigerator until service.

crab ravigote (invigorated crab)

½ cup mayonnaise
4 tablespoons vinegar
¼ cup diced green onion
1 teaspoon capers
2 tablespoons chopped fresh parsley
1 teaspoon tarragon leaves
1 teaspoon Creole mustard †
1 teaspoon Worcestershire sauce
1 teaspoon black pepper
Dash hot sauce
Pinch kosher salt
1 pound lump crabmeat

1. In a large mixing bowl, combine all of the crab ravigote ingredients, except the crabmeat. 2. Gently fold in the lump crabmeat so as not to break up the crab.

frog legs

16 pair frog legs, halved
2 teaspoons kosher salt
2 teaspoons black pepper
1 teaspoon granulated garlic
1 lemon, halved
4 tablespoons extra-virgin olive oil

1. Preheat oven broiler. 2. Lay the frog legs in an oven-safe sauté pan and season with 1 teaspoon salt, 1 teaspoon pepper, garlic, juice from one lemon half and olive oil. Reserve the second half of the lemon. Roll the legs around in the ingredients to coat evenly. 3. Place the sauté pan in the broiler for about 3-4 minutes. Turn the legs over and cook another 3-4 minutes, or until the meat is cooked through. 4. Adjust the seasoning with the remaining salt and pepper.

to plate

1. Divide the Creole tomato slices evenly among 4 plates. 2. Distribute the asparagus spears evenly among the plates on top of the tomato slices. 3. Divide the crab mixture into 4 equal portions and spoon on top of the asparagus. 4. Place 8 broiled legs on each plate, around the crab ravigote. 5. Squeeze the remaining lemon over the frog legs and serve.

*Creole tomatoes are medium-size tomatoes native to New Orleans. Feel free to use your favorite local variety.

†Try Zatarain's Creole mustard, available at most well-stocked grocery stores, online at zatarains.com, at Zydeco's 5 or on our Web site, zydecos.net. You can also use coarse-ground mustard.

serves 6-8

Slice the galette and serve topped with savory Creole cream cheese and a side of braised cabbage

andouille
AND POTATO GALETTE
WITH BRAISED CABBAGE

The galette is a chameleon. It is a quick-change artist, capable of being a sweet dessert or, with just a few changes, a wonderful, savory component of a meal. This galette would be perfect as a main course with an accompanying cold New Orleans dark beer.

pâte brisée (basic pie crust)

- 2 cups flour
- 1 stick (8 tablespoons) butter, frozen and sliced into pats
- Pinch salt
- ½ cup cold water

1. Place 1½ cups flour in a food processor. Add the butter and salt. Pulse once, add the cold water and pulse once more. 2. Dust a work surface with the remaining ½ cup flour. Transfer the dough to the work surface. 3. Shape the dough into a firm ball then flatten it out slightly to make a disk. (Do not knead or overwork the dough.) 4. Wrap the dough in wax paper and let it rest for 30 minutes.

galette

- 4 red new potatoes
- 6 slices bacon
- 2 tablespoons butter
- 2 red onions, peeled and thinly sliced
- 1 green bell pepper, seeded and thinly sliced
- 1 stalk celery, diced
- 4 toes garlic, thinly sliced
- 1 bay leaf
- ½ teaspoon kosher salt
- 1 Pâte Brisée (recipe above)
- Bench flour, as needed
- 1 pound Andouille (recipe on page 23), thinly sliced
- 1 teaspoon red pepper flakes
- 6 fresh sage leaves, chopped
- Paprika, as needed
- Black pepper, as needed
- Creole Cream Cheese (recipe on page 97), to serve

1. Preheat oven to 400 degrees. 2. Boil the potatoes until just cooked through and easily penetrated by a toothpick, about 30 minutes. Drain and let cool. Cut the potatoes into rounds and set aside. 3. In a medium sauté pan, cook the bacon until crisp. Remove and set aside on paper towels to drain. Reserve 2 ounces of bacon grease for the cabbage. 4. Add the butter to the sauté pan. Sauté the trinity (onions, bell pepper and celery) with the garlic, bay leaf and salt for 5 minutes. Remove from heat, drain and set aside. 5. On a lightly floured work surface, roll out the pâte brisée, forming a 9" x 18" rectangle. Gently transfer the dough to a large cookie sheet. 6. Place the sliced andouille on top of the pastry, leaving 2 inches around the edges. Place the trinity mixture on top of the andouille. Sprinkle with red pepper flakes and sage leaves. Lay the slices of potato on top, overlapping slightly. 7. Fold the 2-inch border up and over the outer edge of the toppings. (The middle of the tart will be exposed with a frame of dough around the perimeter.) Sprinkle with paprika and black pepper. 8. Bake in the 400-degree oven for 1 hour or until the crust is golden brown. Brown the galette under a broiler or by using a propane torch to toast for 1 minute. 9. Crumble the bacon over the top.

braised cabbage

- 1 head cabbage
- 2 ounces bacon fat (reserved above)
- 1 teaspoon fennel seed
- 1 cup chicken stock
- 1 pat butter
- Pinch kosher salt
- Pinch black pepper

1. Remove the outer leaves from the cabbage. Cut the cabbage into 8 wedges from top to bottom, through the root end. 2. To a heavy, large sauté pan over high heat, add the bacon fat and fennel seed. Place the cabbage wedges in the sauté pan, cut side down, and cook for 5 minutes. 3. Reduce the heat to medium and cook the cabbage for 5 more minutes, browning the leaves. Flip the cabbage to the other cut side and cook for 5 more minutes. 4. Add the stock and cover. Cook over medium-low heat for 20 minutes, or until most of the liquid has cooked off. 5. Plate, topping each wedge with a pat of butter, a pinch of salt and a pinch of black pepper.

serves 8-10

Drizzle with cane syrup and sprinkle powdered sugar with abandon

lost bread
(PAIN PERDU)

Most people just throw out stale bread, but in New Orleans, we so revere French bread that we wouldn't dream of disposing of it, even if it was stale. Instead, we make a wonderful dish called Pain Perdu, or Lost Bread, and serve it all over the city for Sunday brunch.

crème anglaise

5 egg yolks
⅓ cup sugar
1 vanilla bean
2 cups half-and-half

1. In a medium mixing bowl, combine the egg yolks and sugar. Set aside. 2. Split the vanilla bean and scrape out the interior pulp. Place the bean, pulp and half-and-half in a small saucepan; heat until the contents are very hot but not boiling. 3. Whisk the egg mixture. While whisking, slowly add ½ cup of the hot half-and-half mixture. (This prevents the eggs from scrambling.) 4. Slowly whisk the entire egg and sugar mixture into the remaining half-and-half mixture in the saucepan. Continue to cook until a light custard has formed, about 3-4 minutes. To gauge whether it's done, dip a spoon into the crème anglaise. Draw your finger down the back of the spoon. If the cream coats the back of the spoon and the line stays in place, it is done.

macerated strawberries

1 pound fresh strawberries
¼ cup sugar
1 teaspoon coarse-ground black pepper
Pinch kosher salt
1 teaspoon balsamic vinegar

1. Stem and halve the strawberries. 2. In a medium mixing bowl, combine the sugar, pepper, salt and balsamic vinegar. Add the strawberries. 3. Cover and allow the berries to rest for 15-20 minutes.

lost bread

1 stale French baguette (1-2 days old)
4 eggs
1½ cups milk
1 teaspoon vanilla extract
Pinch allspice
¼ cup sugar
2 tablespoons butter
Crème Anglaise (recipe above)
Macerated Strawberries (recipe above)
½ cup Louisiana cane syrup
Powdered sugar, as needed

1. Cut the French baguette into slices on the bias, about 1-inch thick (about 12 slices). 2. In a medium mixing bowl, combine the eggs, milk, vanilla, allspice and sugar. 3. Place the bread slices into the batter and allow them to soak for 1 minute. 4. As the bread is soaking, place butter in a sauté pan. Heat over medium heat until the butter is melted. 5. Fry the bread slices for about 3 minutes on each side, or until golden brown. Remove the bread from the pan and drain on paper towels. 6. To serve, place a spoonful of crème anglaise on each serving plate. Put 2-3 slices of the lost bread on top of the custard. Place a spoonful of macerated strawberries on top of the bread.

serves 4-6

Garnish the hurricane with cherries and orange wedges.

sazerac

The Sazerac was created by Antoine Amédée Peychaud in New Orleans in the 1800s. It's potent, originally made with French cognac, but today, made with rye whiskey. It's a bit like something your granddad would drink, smoking big cigars, planning to build that railroad across the untamed west or topple the government of some sleepy little country. But they are famous back home and lots of people really like them, so much so that as of 2008, it has been designated by city government decree, "The Official Cocktail of the City of New Orleans." Sazeracs have also been used to remove paint and varnish from wood paneling as well as dissolve bugs and tar from car grills.

1 tablespoon absinthe
2 shots ✱ **Old Overholt Straight Rye Whiskey**
¾ ounce simple syrup ✦
Dash Peychaud's Bitters
Twist of lemon or 1 cherry, to garnish

1. To a rocks or old fashioned glass, add the absinthe and swirl around to coat the interior of the glass. Dump out any excess absinthe. **2.** In a cocktail shaker, stir to combine the rye whiskey and simple syrup. **3.** Fill the rocks or old fashioned glass with ice. Pour in the whiskey mixture. **4.** Add a dash of bitters and garnish with a twist of lemon or a cherry.

(serves 1)

✱ *A shot or jigger equals 1½ ounces.*

✦ *To make simple syrup, dissolve 2 packets of sugar in ¾ ounce of water.*

hurricane*

It's one of the most famous drinks ever created and known throughout the civilized world. It's the Hurricane, a mixture of fruit juice and rum steeped in New Orleans history. The name comes from the shape of the glass in which it's served, which is sort of fat at the bottom and flaring up and out at the top similar to an old hurricane lantern. There are many variations. I can remember making them in college when the only thing we had was fruit punch concentrate and what I believe was rum made out of old tires, all served up in Styrofoam cups. Not the best recipe, so I won't give that one here. I will, however, give you the dynamite version we make at The Z. We sell gallons of them to rave reviews. Here then, and for the first time ever, is our own secret recipe for a Zydeco Hurricane.

16 ounces ✦ **cranberry juice**
16 ounces pineapple juice
16 ounces white rum
16 ounces gold or dark rum
16 ounces coconut rum
2 shots grenadine
16 ounces sour mix, to taste
Cherries, to garnish
Orange wedges, to garnish

1. Combine all of the ingredients, except the cherries and orange wedges, in a 1 gallon jug. **2.** Refrigerate until ice cold and serve in hurricane glasses with crushed ice.

(makes 1 gallon)

✱ *As is true with cooking, the quality of the finished product is only as good as its ingredients. Use the best quality juices and rum you can find.*

✦ *A shot or jigger equals 1½ ounces.*

Tuck the cherry bounce away in a cool, dry place for 6 months or longer

cherry BOUNCE

My Cajun grandfather made the best bounce, using tiny wild berries and whiskey. He kept a jar way in the back of his closet and only brought it out for weddings and funerals. I am going to give you the recipe as it was given to me, with minimum alterations. Bounce is a wonderful aperitif. Sip it slowly. It warms the soul.

A glass jar with lid
Fresh cherries, stemmed and halved, with pits
Vodka or whiskey
Cane sugar
6 months of your time

1. Fill a large glass jar halfway full with cherries and pits. Add your favorite vodka or whiskey, leaving space at the top for the sugar. Add 2 cups of sugar for every 1 liter of alcohol. Top off the jar and screw on the lid.

(makes 1 jar)

absinthe (THE GREEN FAIRY)

Nothing compares to absinthe when it comes to a charged name and a checkered past. The scourge of civilized society, this green fairy is conjured up from some scary place, made by smelly orcs and trolls. One glass and you'll instantly go insane, jump out of a window, kick a puppy or trip a nun. On Bourbon Street, you pass The Old Absinthe House, where glasses of the evil drink were dispensed until civil servants with official metal clipboards banned it for the good of society.

The hysterics have subsided and you can buy it in the States again. We serve it at Zydeco's because of its ties to New Orleans and high demand. To be honest, it's really not great. If you don't like licorice, you won't like it. I love licorice but I don't like absinthe. I guess it's the name, hardware, ceremony, history and untold fanciful naughty taboos that attribute for its draw. I would kill for that kind of press at the Z.

There are two methods for serving absinthe. The Bohemian method is a bit on the theatrical side, involving fire, circus clowns and flea-ridden monkeys wearing fezzes. I prefer the more sedate, traditional way.

2 ounces * absinthe
1 absinthe glass or glass tumbler
1 absinthe spoon or regular fork
1 sugar cube
4 ounces ice-cold water

1. Pour the absinthe into an absinthe glass or glass tumbler. 2. Hold the absinthe spoon or fork over the glass. Put the sugar cube on the utensil. 3. Slowly pour the water over the sugar and allow the water to flow into the glass. Drop any remaining sugar in the absinthe and stir gently. The green absinthe will turn a milky white, a process known as "a louche." 4. Locate the nearest nun, puppy or window and have fun.

(serves 1)

*A shot or jigger equals 1 1/2 ounces.

chapter 3

The bawdy, in-your-face alligator sauce piquant is a recipe easily considered part of the cornerstone of the cuisine of south Louisiana.

THE OLD SQUARE (VIEUX CARRÉ)
WHAT CAN I SAY?

The Vieux Carré, the Old Square, Jackson Square, the French Quarter, the original city of New Orleans. What did those early New Orleanians eat? My best educated guess would be the dishes featured in this chapter. Some of these define the city. Some date back to the earliest south Louisiana settlers.

In this chapter, you will find the simplicity of country cooking, the thick and complex metropolitan taste of a really good seafood gumbo, the simple beauty of pairing tomato and shrimp in a Creole, the bawdy, in-your-face alligator sauce piquant.

These recipes and others could arguably be considered part of the cornerstone of the cuisine of south Louisiana. I have old, local cookbooks from early-last century, in which these dishes are prominently featured. They haven't changed all that much over the years. If something works, you don't have to fix it.

This is the food my mother made, her mother, her father, their parents. The dishes can be found in any Louisiana restaurant worth its salt. They are recipes where it is better to just go ahead and make them rather than have me try to explain what they are. Sometimes words just don't work. I have been sitting here in front of this computer over the course of several days trying to write something that isn't maudlin or corny or trite. I have never been one at a loss for words, yet...

I have been trying to pull something out of the core of my being and put it down on paper, but I can't do it. I give. The Old Square stares Hutch down! There are no stories from my past, no platitudes, no clichés that will work for this introduction. This is just too big and I am too little to convey it to you. You need to make these recipes for yourself and then you can find your own words. It wouldn't be a real Zydeco's cookbook unless I showed you how to make them. I know I can show you how to make them. It's the best I can do. It's all I can do.

To plate, spoon alligator meat mixture over white rice and sprinkle with 1 tablespoon red pepper flakes and garnish with dill fronds.

golden alligator
SAUCE PIQUANT
(COCODRIE PIQUANT D'OR)

What to do when you have a date with your best girl in 30 minutes and there is an alligator lounging beneath your '74 yellow Ford Pinto with avocado-hued interior? Well, that was the situation I found myself in one memorable day. ∗ Alligators have cold, dead eyes that can pierce your soul and, if you aren't careful, ruin a perfectly good time. As I traversed down the bayou in my pirogue, I always gave gators the respect they deserve, allowing them a wide berth. This guy, however, wanted to ride shotgun on my date. ∗ To be honest, alligators have always scared the crap out of me. My cousins and uncles have no such flaw, and are more than happy to help dispatch any wayward reptile back to the Cretaceous period. A quick phone call resulted in what can only be described as an impromptu family reunion, with the gator as the guest of honor. ∗ With impressive speed and dexterity, the alligator was successfully extricated and carried off with great fanfare by my whooping cousins. And, with that, I left for my date. The next day, a package of fresh alligator meat was in the fridge. It was my portion of the bounty after it was split among the participants of the previous day's festivities. ∗ Here is a beautiful Acadiana dish, dedicated to my cousins and Monsieur Cocodrie. This spicy alligator sauce piquant is special in that it incorporates yellow tomatoes, carrots, black olives and a blond roux.

serves 6-8

- 1 cup extra-virgin olive oil
- 1 cup flour
- 1 cup minced carrot
- 1 cup diced yellow onion
- 1 cup pitted, drained whole kalamata or niçoise olives
- 2 cups seeded, diced yellow bell peppers
- 1 tablespoon kosher salt
- 1 teaspoon black pepper
- ½ teaspoon celery seed
- ½ teaspoon cayenne
- ½ teaspoon plus 1 tablespoon red pepper flakes
- 8 yellow tomatoes, blanched, peeled and diced
- 1 bay leaf
- ½ cup Shrimp Stock (recipe on page 13)
- 4 toes garlic, minced
- 2 tablespoons fresh dill, stems removed and chopped, plus more to garnish
- 1 teaspoon hot sauce
- 2 pounds cleaned alligator tail meat ∗, all fat and membranes removed, cubed
- White rice, cooked, to serve

1. In a small saucepan over medium heat, mix the oil and flour to make a white roux (about 5 minutes).
2. Sauté the carrot, onion, olives and bell pepper in the roux for about 5 minutes. Add the salt, black pepper, celery seed, cayenne and ½ teaspoon red pepper flakes. Cook until the onions are translucent, about 10 minutes.
3. Add the tomatoes, bay leaf, stock, garlic, dill, hot sauce and alligator meat. Bring the mixture to a strong simmer.
4. Reduce the heat and cook at a low simmer for 1 hour, stirring often.

∗ To source alligator meat, call your local butcher, check online, stop into Zydeco's 5 or order at zydecos.net

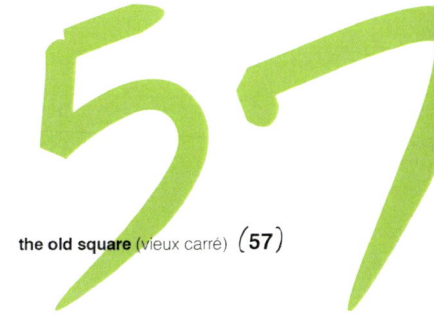

Top each crawfish pie with green onion and paprika. Se and enjoy!

crawfish pie

There are entire symphonies written about crawfish pie. Well, OK, I think there is maybe one song somewhere that mentions it. Anyway, here is my favorite crawfish pie recipe and there should be a song written about it. It has tons of crawfish tail meat, andouille and cheese. It has heavy cream, corn, wine and butter, carbohydrates and fat galore and it has a whole bunch of crawfish on top to scare the kids and neighbors. If you try to jam anything else in here, I think it will explode in some kind of stupendous chain reaction. I wouldn't recommend anyone eat like this everyday, of course, but just this once, treat yourself to a classic New Orleans dish. Serve with a nice, light spinach salad and a cold diet drink to alleviate the guilt.

serves 4

pâte brisée (basic crust)

- 3½ cups flour
- 2 sticks butter, frozen and sliced into pats
- Pinch salt
- ½ cup cold water

1. Place 3 cups of flour into a food processor. Add the butter and salt and pulse on and off 2 times. **2.** Add the chilled water and pulse a final time. **3.** Use the remaining flour to lightly dust a work surface. Transfer the dough to the work area. Form and press the dough into a ball, then flatten it out slightly to make a disk. (Do not knead or overwork the dough.) **4.** Wrap the dough in wax paper and allow it to rest for 30 minutes.

pie filling

- 1 Pâte Brisée (recipe above)
- 1 ear of corn
- 1 cup diced onion
- ½ cup diced celery
- 1 cup diced green bell pepper
- 1 tablespoon dried thyme leaves
- 3 toes garlic, minced
- 1 teaspoon salt
- 1 teaspoon black pepper
- 1 bay leaf
- 4 tablespoons butter
- 1 tablespoon tomato paste
- 1 tablespoon hot sauce
- ¼ cup heavy cream
- 1 pound boiled crawfish tail meat (Crawfish Boil recipe on page 83)
- 2 cups Shrimp Stock (recipe on page 13)
- 1 pound boiled red potatoes, cubed
- ½ cup dry white wine
- 3 tablespoons flour
- 1 pound Andouille sausage (recipe on page 23), cubed
- 1 pound whole boiled crawfish (Crawfish Boil recipe on page 83)
- 1 pound shredded mozzarella cheese
- ½ cup diced green onion
- 1 tablespoon paprika

1. Preheat oven to 350 degrees. **2.** On a lightly floured surface, quarter the prepared pâte brisée dough and roll it out into 4 equal rounds. Place the pastry in 4 ovenproof soup bowls; allow the dough to hang over the edge of each bowl. Tear the dough around the bowls, making a decorative edge. **3.** Blind bake the pastry crusts in the 350-degree oven for 20 minutes or until golden brown. **4.** Scrape or cut the corn kernels off of the cob into a small bowl. Set aside. **5.** In a large sauté pan, sauté the onion, celery, bell pepper, thyme, garlic, salt, pepper and bay leaf in 4 tablespoons of butter. Add the tomato paste and cook for 1 minute. **6.** Add the corn, hot sauce and cream and simmer for 3 minutes. **7.** Add the crawfish tail meat and simmer for 1 minute. **8.** Add the shrimp stock, potatoes and wine and bring back to a simmer. **9.** Sprinkle the flour over the mixture, cover with a lid and cook for 3 minutes. **10.** Remove the bay leaf and stir. The mixture should have a thick consistency. If not, continue to simmer with the lid off until it thickens up. Stir in the andouille. **11.** Preheat the broiler. **12.** Spoon the mixture into the blind-baked pastry bowls. Cover with whole crawfish and shredded cheese. Brown the bowls under a broiler until the cheese is hot and bubbly.

Combine the red beans with sausage and the jazzed-up rice in one dish for an unforgettable Louisiana meal.

red beans AND RICE WITH SAUSAGE

Traditionally served every Monday, red beans and rice have been a New Orleans favorite from the earliest days of the city. Thick slices of sausage and pickled meat swirl in smoky red kidney beans topped with long-grain white rice. It is one of those dishes that defines south Louisiana. I wouldn't consider it a proper Monday if I couldn't have a bowl of red beans and rice with sausage for lunch.

red beans

- 2 pounds Camellia brand dried red kidney beans *
- 2 quarts plus 12 cups water
- 2 cups Spanish onion, brunoise
- 1 cup finely diced celery
- 3 cups green bell pepper, seeded, 1-inch dice
- ¼ cup vegetable oil
- 3 toes garlic, sliced
- 1 tablespoon dried thyme leaves
- 1 bay leaf
- 1 tablespoon fresh-cracked black pepper
- ½ teaspoon cayenne
- 3 tablespoons kosher salt
- 8 ounces Pickled Meat (recipe on page 33)
- 2 pounds smoked sausage or Andouille (recipe on page 33)
- 3 tablespoons Worcestershire sauce
- 1 teaspoon liquid smoke
- 1 tablespoon Crystal brand hot sauce +
- 1 stick butter

1. Carefully pick through the beans, removing any stones, and rinse the beans thoroughly. Place the beans in a large, clean bowl with 2 quarts of cool, fresh water. Allow the beans to soak in the refrigerator overnight. Drain the next day. **2.** In the bottom of a 4-quart stockpot, sauté the onion, celery and bell pepper in the vegetable oil for 5 minutes or until the onions are translucent. **3.** Add the garlic and continue to cook for 1 minute. **4.** Add the thyme, bay leaf, pepper, cayenne and drained beans. Add 12 cups of water, salt, pickled meat, sausage, Worcestershire, liquid smoke and hot sauce. Bring to a boil. **5.** Reduce the heat to medium, stirring occasionally. Cook over medium heat at a simmer until the beans begin to burst and the liquid becomes thick, about 2-2½ hours. Stir occasionally, scraping the bottom so the beans do not stick. **6.** Just before serving, add the butter, adjust seasonings and remove the bay leaf.

jazzed-up rice

- 4 cups duck or chicken stock
- 2 cups long-grain rice

1. Add the stock and rice to a large stockpot and bring to a boil. **2.** Reduce the heat to medium-low and allow the rice to cook until all of the stock has evaporated, 30-45 minutes. **3.** Gently fluff the rice using a spoon or fork and serve.

* You can find Camellia products in many well-stocked grocery stores, at camelliabrand.com, at Zydeco's 5 or on our Web site, zydecos.net

+ You can find Crystal brand hot sauce in many well-stocked grocery stores, online at crystalhotsauce.com, at Zydeco's 5 or on our Web site, zydecos.net

serves 8

the old square (vieux carré) (61)

Serve with white rice, sliced lemon and a sprinkle of gumbo filé. As with any gumbo, seafood gumbo is better the next day

seafood gumbo

Whole gumbo crab, alligator sausage, gulf shrimp, crawfish tail meat. Is there any dish more identified with New Orleans than a really good seafood gumbo? I think not. It is more than a soup, more than the sum of its parts, it has hundreds of years of history behind it, songs have been written about it and well, it's just damn good.

- 1 cup extra-virgin olive oil
- 1 cup flour
- 1 cup diced onion
- ½ cup diced celery
- 2 cups diced green, yellow and red bell peppers
- ½ tablespoon salt
- 1 sprig fresh thyme
- 1 bay leaf
- 1 tablespoon black pepper
- ½ teaspoon cayenne
- 2 tablespoons tomato paste
- 2 cups sliced okra
- 1 pound Alligator Sausage (recipe on page 29) *
- 4 toes garlic, diced
- 4 cups Shrimp Stock (recipe on page 13)
- 3 cups white wine
- 4 cups whole tomatoes, in juice, crushed
- 1 tablespoon hot sauce
- 2 pounds 26-30-count shrimp, peeled and deveined
- 1 pound gumbo crabs *, halved
- 2 dozen select oysters, liquor reserved
- 1 pound crawfish tail meat *
- 1 cup diced green onion
- 1 cup chopped fresh parsley
- 8 cups cooked white rice
- Lemon slices, to garnish
- Sprinkle gumbo file +, to garnish

1. In an 8-quart Dutch oven or stockpot, stir the oil and flour over medium heat until a medium-brown roux is achieved, about 1 hour. 2. Add the onion, celery, bell peppers, salt, thyme, bay leaf, black pepper and cayenne and cook for 10 minutes. 3. Add the tomato paste and cook for 2 minutes. 4. Add the okra and cook for 5 minutes. 5. Add the alligator sausage and cook for 5 minutes. 6. Add the garlic, shrimp stock, white wine, 16 ounces tomatoes and hot sauce. Cover and simmer for 30 minutes. 7. Add the shrimp, crab, remaining 16 ounces tomatoes, oyster liquor and crawfish and simmer for 20 minutes. 8. Remove from heat and add the oysters, green onion and parsley. Allow the gumbo to rest for 15 minutes; remove bay leaf.

* Gumbo crabs, crawfish and other Louisiana items can be purchased online at Bayou Bounty, a store out of Boutte. bayoubountyseafood.com. Another good source is Kyle LeBlanc Crawfish Farms, klcrawfishfarms.com. You can also stop into Zydeco's 5 or order at zydecos.net.

+ Gumbo file (fee-lay) is ground sassafras leaves. It is used to thicken and flavor gumbos and soups. Try Zatarain's version, available at well-stocked grocery stores. zatarains.com. Zydeco's 5 or on our Web site, zydecos.net.

serves 8-10

Serve with white rice, garlic bread and a sprinkling of basil and marjoram over top.

shrimp creole

Against an ancient and crumbling red brick courtyard wall, water from a small fountain bubbles up through layers of frilled, blue lichen and thick, green moss. A bronze water nymph dutifully directs the cool artesian water down into a verdigris basin. The subtle yet sharp smell of fresh Creole tomatoes slow cooking swirls in the humid air. It traverses the narrow adjacent kitchen and is carried up and out through cypress doors into the Spanish courtyard. Large shrimp co-mingle with the tomato, sautéed and savory and served atop mounds of white rice and a side of herbed garlic bread. Scents of basil, garlic and perfumed marjoram playfully dance against the courtyard's fragrant sweet olive and magnolia tree air. In the distance, the cathedral's Sunday bells echo down the rue. It is truly the perfect dish. The perfect setting. It is truly simple and elegant.

garlic bread

- 1 French bread bâtard
- 2 tablespoons minced garlic
- 1 teaspoon black pepper
- 1 tablespoon chopped fresh marjoram
- ¼ cup grated Parmesan cheese
- 2 tablespoons chopped fresh parsley
- 1 stick butter, room temperature and softened

1. Preheat oven to 350 degrees. **2.** Cut the bâtard in half horizontally down the middle. **3.** In a medium mixing bowl, fold the garlic, pepper, marjoram, cheese and parsley in with the butter. **4.** Spread the butter mixture over each half of the bâtard. **5.** Put the halves back together. Wrap the bâtard in aluminum foil and bake in the 350-degree oven for 30 minutes. **6.** Remove the bread from the foil. Tear into large pieces and serve with the Creole.

creole

- 1 cup diced onion
- 1 cup diced celery
- 2 cups seeded, diced green bell pepper
- 4 toes garlic, sliced
- 1 bay leaf
- 4 tablespoons tomato paste
- 1 tablespoon kosher salt
- 1 tablespoon black pepper
- 1 tablespoon hot sauce
- 4 Creole tomatoes *, blanched, cored and diced
- ½ cup Shrimp Stock (recipe on page 13)
- 1 tablespoon chiffonade fresh basil
- 1 tablespoon chiffonade fresh marjoram

1. In a medium saucepan, sauté the onion, celery, bell pepper, garlic and bay leaf until the onions are translucent, about 5 minutes. **2.** Add the tomato paste, salt, pepper and hot sauce and cook for 5 minutes, stirring often. **3.** Add the diced tomato, shrimp stock, basil and marjoram. Cover and cook over medium heat for 25 minutes, stirring occasionally.

shrimp

- 2 pounds 26-30-count raw tiger shrimp
- 2 tablespoons extra-virgin olive oil
- 2 teaspoons kosher salt
- 2 teaspoons black pepper
- 1 tablespoon thyme leaves
- 2 tablespoons Worcestershire sauce
- 1 teaspoon paprika
- 1 teaspoon hot sauce
- 1 lemon, halved
- Cooked white rice, to serve
- Garlic Bread (recipe above), to serve
- 1 tablespoon chiffonade fresh basil, to serve
- 1 tablespoon chiffonade fresh marjoram, to serve

1. Clean and peel the shrimp. Set aside. **2.** Pour the extra-virgin olive oil into a large, hot sauté pan. When it just begins to smoke, add the salt, pepper, thyme, Worcestershire sauce, paprika and hot sauce. Squeeze the lemon halves and drop them into the pan. Add the peeled shrimp and stir once. Sauté for 2 minutes. **3.** Gently turn the shrimp and sauté for 1 minute or until the shrimp are just pink. (Do not overcook the shrimp.) **4.** Combine the shrimp mixture and Creole and cook for an additional 5 minutes.

serves 4

*Creole tomatoes are medium tomatoes that were developed to survive the warm, humid climate of the south. They're very popular in south Louisiana, but if they don't stock them at your local farmers market, use any fresh, local variety.

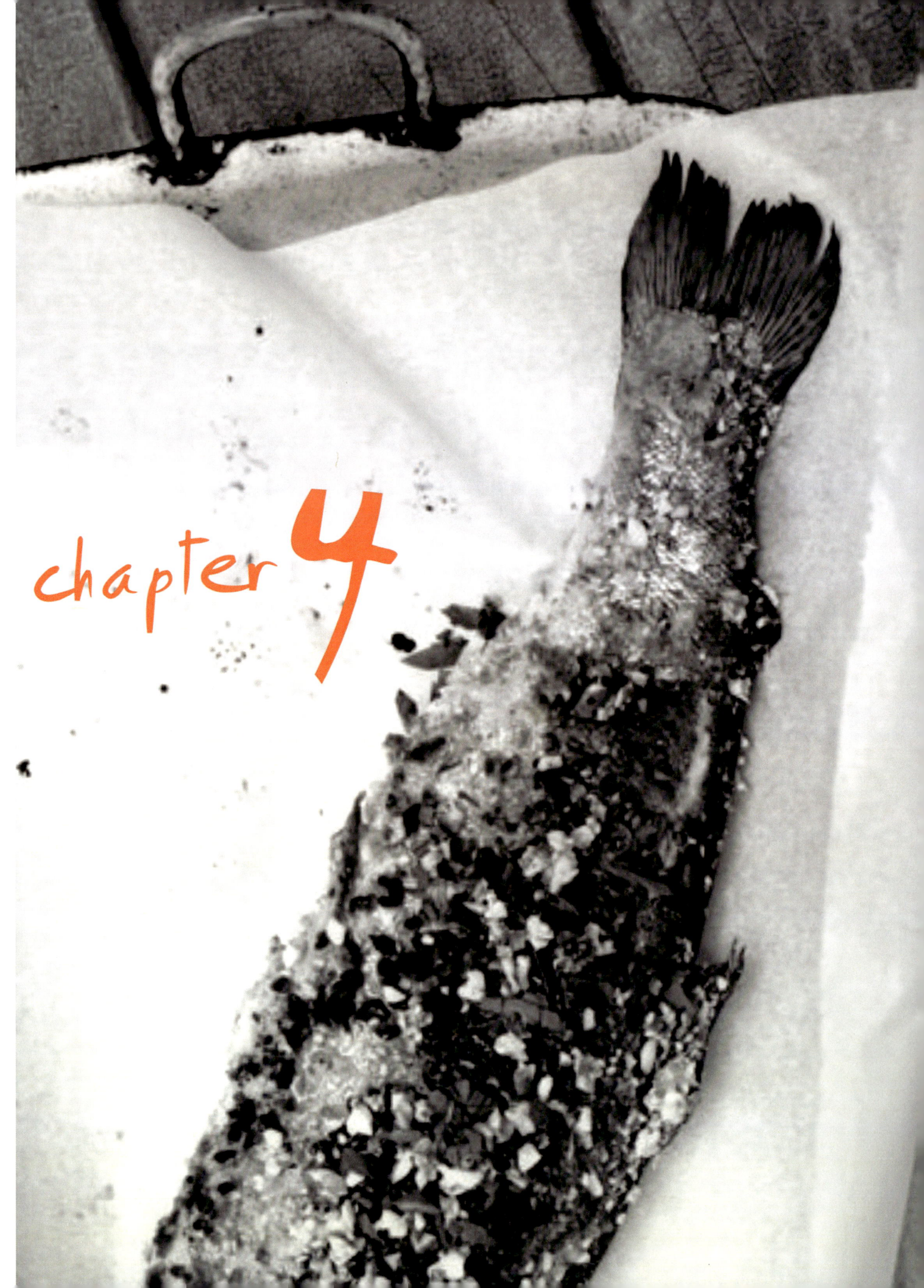

chapter 4

FISH + SEAFOOD (FRUITS DE MER)
"IF GOD IS A CRUSTACEAN, I'M TOTALLY SCREWED."

With thousands of miles of tidal shoreline including intricate backwater bayous, waterways, lakes, ponds, primordial streams and cyprieres (Cypress swamps), seafood is bound to play a big role in the cuisine and culture of south Louisiana. When culinary skills from a myriad of cultural influences meet mythical bayou and gulf-water beasties that are reverently mixed, blended, folded, skinned, scaled, refined, not refined, simultaneously simple and complex, magic happens.

Forget about the steamed blandness of supermarket shrimp, their line upon row of perfect soldiers in little plastic rings, ironically as devoid of flavor as they are perfect in appearance. You instinctively dowse them in cocktail sauce, any sauce, where the hell is the sauce? Why? Because these shrimp have the flavor profile of wet cotton. It's like boiling a filet mignon and attempting to salvage it with ketchup; misguided, pointless and a crime. Yes, shun the mediocrity of drive-through, deep-fried, fish-shaped Styrofoam jetsam and flotsam served in a happy box. Rebuke spray painted faux crab-meat, because it's lying to you and you shouldn't have to take that from your food. Turn away from popcorn shrimp (I have a name for popcorn shrimp: crumbs). And the precooked, frozen crab legs and fish nuggets? What the hell is a fish nugget?

However, there is reason to rejoice my brothers and sisters. Come over to the dark side; the place your mother warned you about but secretly wanted to go. It is where Kermit and his cousins lose their legs and roll around the swamp in little wheelchairs. Where your upcoming dinner is under your pirogue (thinking you are its upcoming dinner). Where long, sharp blades pry open mud-encrusted shells revealing beautiful, salty, live oysters. Where the screams of a thousand crawfish are silenced as they are plunged into boiling pots of cayenne-infused soup. Where seasoning and skill from far-away lands merge with local invention and are used with abandon and great results. Where eyes and heads and legs and tails are used to create voodoo magic on your plate. It's life, it's cooking, it's real seafood.

Walk into a seafood shack in Abbeville and feast upon large metal trays of steaming Vermillion Bay blue crabs just plucked from a swirling, spicy cauldron. Saunter into a Thibodaux restaurant and order the all-you-can-eat crawfish deal. Drive up to Madisonville and get a stuffed red snapper that will blow you away. Stumble into a little place at the corner of Carrolton and St. Charles and get a couple dozen oysters. Or take that short trip to a little shack on the Mississippi River that has the best alligator po'boy on the planet.

I have traveled to the dark side. Actually, I was lucky enough to be born there, to live and love there. I have pried open thick shells revealing salty morsels of heaven. I have boiled shrimp with, (God, yes), heads and tails and antennas and feasted on their perfectly cooked bodies. I have pried open crabs like some sort of demented Christmas present with claws. I have sucked the heads of a million crawfish. I've killed hundreds of thousands of them and prepared them in a multitude of ways – crawfish bisque, boiled crawfish, crawfish étouffée, fried crawfish, crawfish Creole – the list is endless. I am amazed at the different and flavorful ways they can be elevated to greatness. Much respect and props to my little red and green bayou brothers, but I can't help thinking, "If God is a crustacean, I'm screwed."

Yes, it's all of this and more. Differing locales, different ways of approaching the dish, a polyglot of cultures and peoples all coming together and making the best food that can be made. If you're looking for the recipe for fish sticks and ketchup you just saw on the Cookery Channel, just put this book down and back away slowly, because now you are scaring me. If, however, you want to try something that will get you closer to that Abbeville café, the Thibodaux restaurant or that little shack on the Mississippi River, then dear reader, please read on.

Plate the catfish and serve with equal portions of the dirty rice and orange salad.

catfish pecandine
AND DIRTY RICE
WITH BLOOD ORANGE, OLIVE AND RED ONION SALAD

This is the Louisiana Creole variation of the classic French dish Trout Almondine, which goes back to the earliest days of New Orleans. Here, I encrust catfish with crushed pecans and then lightly fry the filets in browned butter. Pecans are abundant in south Louisiana and find their way into a great deal of the area's recipes. Cajun dirty rice and an orange, olive and red onion salad, a nod to the time when south Louisiana was a Spanish territory and New Orleans was its capitol, are both a nice complement to the rich entree.

dirty rice

Gizzards, livers, necks, wings and backbones of 2 chickens or ducks (or 3 cups chicken livers and gizzards)
1 toe garlic, crushed
1 tablespoon kosher salt
1 bay leaf
6 cups water
1 tablespoon chicken base
¾ cup bacon, diced
4 tablespoons butter
2 cups white rice
1 cup diced onion
½ cup diced celery
1 cup diced green bell pepper
1 teaspoon dried thyme
1 teaspoon paprika
1 teaspoon black pepper

1. Place giblets, garlic, salt and bay leaf in a large stockpot. Add the water and bring mixture to a boil. Boil on low for 30 minutes, skimming off any scum that rises to the surface. **2.** Strain the mixture and reserve the stock in the pot. Add water if necessary to bring the total volume to 4 cups. **3.** Add the chicken base to the stock. Cover and bring the stock back up to a slow simmer. Set stock aside. (Makes about 1½-2 cups.) **4.** Pull any meat from the bones and discard. Dice the gizzards and livers. Set aside. **5.** In a large saucepan, cook the diced bacon in the butter for 2 minutes. Add the rice and cook 2 additional minutes to brown. **6.** Add the onion, celery, bell pepper, thyme, paprika and black pepper. Cook for 5 minutes, scraping from the bottom often. **7.** Add the diced meat and reserved stock to the vegetable mixture, and bring to a boil. Stir and reduce heat to medium so that the rice is at a low simmer. Cover and cook until most of the liquid has evaporated and the rice is fully cooked, about 25 minutes.

blood orange, olive and red onion salad

3 blood oranges
1 small red onion
4 ounces pitted empeltre or kalamata olives
3 sprigs flat leaf parsley, chopped
3 tablespoons extra-virgin olive oil
1 teaspoon kosher salt
2 teaspoons black pepper

1. Using a microgater, zest the oranges to make about 1 tablespoon of zest. Peel the remaining skin and divide the oranges into segments. **2.** Peel and thinly slice the red onion. Soak the onions in ice water for 30 minutes, then drain. **3.** In a large mixing bowl, gently combine the orange segments, orange zest, olives, parsley, red onion, olive oil, salt and pepper. Set aside until service.

catfish pecandine

1 cup milk
1 tablespoon Tabasco sauce
½ cup Creole mustard *
4 catfish filets
2 cups finely chopped pecans
1 tablespoon dried parsley
1 teaspoon dried thyme
½ cup flour
1 stick butter
Salt, to taste
Dirty Rice (recipe above), to serve
Blood Orange, Olive and Red Onion Salad (recipe above), to serve

1. In a medium mixing bowl, combine the milk, Tabasco and Creole mustard. Soak the catfish in the mixture for 30 minutes. **2.** In a deep plate, mix the pecans, parsley, thyme and flour. Drain the catfish and dredge in the pecan mixture. **3.** In a large cast-iron skillet or sauté pan, heat the butter until it begins to brown. Add the catfish and fry for 4-5 minutes per side, or until golden brown. **4.** Remove the catfish to drain on a paper towel-lined plate. Add salt, to taste.

*Try Zatarain's Creole mustard, available at most well-stocked grocery stores, or online at zatarains.com, at Zydeco's $ or on our Web site, zydecos.net

serves 4

fish and seafood (fruits de mer)

Top with the tomato and avocado or place the remoulade on the side, and serve garnished with a lemon wedge.

fried "bustah" CRABS WITH TOMATO AND AVOCADO REMOULADE

I love serving this dish at The Z for a number of reasons. Back home, you purchase crabs from a large box as they scuttle about with cool water running over them under the beautiful blue Louisiana sky. Harvesters walk up and down the rows of boxes, scanning for "da' bustahs" (the busters), crabs in molt, busting out of their old shells. As they grow, crabs must molt. They must shed their old, small shells and expand. Over time, the new shell hardens and protects the crab from its predators. For a brief time between molts, the crab has a very soft exterior. Not so much of a shell but more like a thin, soft skin. * Bustahs are harvested, cleaned, fried up and sent out to scare the unsuspecting. When large, angry fried crabs with their legs and their menacing claws all akimbo, are presented to the customer, well, it's great fun to watch their expressions. * I love this job.

serves 6

crab

- 2 quarts peanut oil
- 2 cups flour
- 4 eggs, whisked
- 1 tablespoon plus 1 teaspoon hot sauce
- 4 cups fresh bread crumbs
- 1 teaspoon black pepper
- 2 teaspoons dried thyme
- 1 Creole tomato, diced *
- 3 ripe avocados, peeled, seeded and cubed
- Pinch kosher salt
- 2 lemons, sliced into wedges
- 1 tablespoon extra-virgin olive oil
- 1 cup mayonnaise
- 1 cup ketchup
- 1 hard-boiled egg, chopped
- 1 teaspoon capers
- 1 tablespoon Worcestershire sauce
- ¼ cup diced green onion
- 1 teaspoon grated horseradish
- Pinch cayenne pepper
- 1 teaspoon granulated garlic
- Pinch white pepper
- 6 jumbo soft-shell crabs
- 1 head romaine lettuce, shredded

1. In a 4-quart stockpot, heat the peanut oil to 365-375 degrees. **2.** Using 3 trays or shallow bowls, set up a frying station. In the first tray, place the flour. In the second tray, put the whisked eggs and 1 tablespoon of hot sauce. In the third tray, put the bread crumbs, black pepper and thyme. **3.** In a small bowl, gently fold together the diced tomato and avocado. Incorporate kosher salt, 1 tablespoon of lemon juice (extracted from wedges) and 1 tablespoon of olive oil. Set aside. **4.** In a medium bowl, mix the mayonnaise, ketchup, hard-boiled egg, capers, Worcestershire sauce, green onion, horseradish, cayenne, granulated garlic, white pepper and 1 teaspoon hot sauce. Set aside. **5.** Dredge each crab first in the flour, then the eggs and finally the breading. **6.** Using a pair of kitchen tongs, gently hold the crab from the back so that the legs and claws are facing away from you. Slowly and carefully slide the crab into the heated peanut oil, pushing forward so that the legs and claws spread out. Fry each crab for 2 minutes. Flip over and fry for an additional 2-3 minutes or until golden brown. Drain on paper towels. **7.** To plate, place a handful of shredded romaine lettuce on the center of a plate. Place a fried crab on top of the lettuce. Spoon the remoulade (the mayonnaise mixture) around the crab. +

*Creole tomatoes are a medium-size tomato native to New Orleans. If you can't find them at your farmers market, use your favorite local variety.

+Typically served as a po'boy at south Louisiana restaurants, this version of fried soft-shell crabs is served as a light lunch with a wonderful remoulade.

Sprinkle the shrimp and potatoes with red pepper seeds, and garnish with chopped parsley and lemon slices.

shrimp baronne
(THE BARONESS' SHRIMP)

I had a version of this seafood dish in a little place just outside of Lee Circle, New Orleans. It is surprising in that this recipe pairs shrimp with potatoes, a combination not often seen. A wonderful and spicy tomato-based sauce holds it all together and offers a little punch.

sauce baronne

- 1 32-ounce can whole tomatoes, drained
- 1 cup chopped onions
- 3 tablespoons extra-virgin olive oil
- 2 tablespoons tomato paste
- ⅔ cup dark brown sugar
- ½ cup vinegar
- ½ teaspoon salt
- ½ tablespoon paprika
- ½ tablespoon cayenne
- ½ tablespoon granulated garlic
- 1 tablespoon hot sauce
- 1 cup vegetable oil

1. Puree the tomatoes in a food processor until smooth. **2.** In a medium sauté pan over medium heat, cook the onions in olive oil for 5 minutes. Add the tomato paste and cook for another 1 minute. Add the tomatoes and all of the remaining ingredients, except the vegetable oil, and cook at a low simmer for 1 hour. Stir often to prevent scorching. Remove from heat and allow the mixture to cool. **3.** Transfer the mixture to a food processor or blender and combine. With the motor running, slowly drizzle in the 1 cup of vegetable oil and blend until smooth.

Makes about 3 cups

shrimp baronne

- 3 pounds red potatoes
- 4 tablespoons extra-virgin olive oil
- 2 pounds 26-30-count raw shrimp, peeled and deveined
- 3 cups Sauce Baronne (recipe above)
- 1 teaspoon red pepper seeds, to garnish
- Chopped fresh parsley, to garnish
- Lemon slices, to garnish

1. Preheat oven to 350 degrees. **2.** Boil the potatoes until cooked through, about 30-40 minutes. Drain, cool and cut the potatoes into ¾-inch dice. **3.** To a large ovenproof sauté pan set over medium-high heat, add the extra-virgin olive oil and brown the potatoes, about 5 minutes per side. **4.** In a large mixing bowl, combine the shrimp and the sauce baronne. **5.** Place the shrimp in with the browned potatoes; pour any sauce drippings over the top of the shrimp/potato mixture. **6.** Bake in the 350-degree oven for 15-20 minutes.

serves 4-6

To serve, squeeze fresh lemon juice over the fish. Garnish with dill fronds and eat immediately.

speckled trout
STUFFED WITH CRAWFISH

The pairing of succulent Louisiana crawfish with speckled trout creates a truly memorable meal. This follows the great New Orleans culinary tradition of shoving mass quantities of fresh seafood into something else, thereby creating a whole greater than the individual parts. In the art world this is known as "gestalt". In the culinary arts, it adds a rich flavor component. In other words, we would say, "it just tastes great." Drizzle liberally with extra-virgin olive oil and a squeeze of freshly cut lemon. I would serve this dish with grilled asparagus and hollandaise, fresh baby leaf spinach or roasted mirliton.

crawfish dressing

½ stick butter
1 cup finely diced onions
1 cup finely diced carrots
1 cup finely diced celery
1 teaspoon salt
1 teaspoon black pepper
Pinch cayenne
1 pound crawfish tail meat
½ cup diced green onion
2 toes garlic, sliced
¼ cup fresh parsley, chopped
1 egg
½ cup bread crumbs

1. In a medium sauté pan over medium heat, melt the butter. Add the onions, carrots, celery, salt, pepper and cayenne, and cook for 5 minutes, stirring occasionally. 2. Add the crawfish tail meat and cook, stirring often, for 2 minutes. Add the green onion, garlic and parsley and continue to cook for 1 minute. 3. Pour the mixture into a medium mixing bowl and cool for about 5 minutes. 4. Add the egg and bread crumbs and mix well. Set aside.

trout

3 cups flour
2 cups buttermilk
4 tablespoons Creole mustard *
Pinch cayenne
1 teaspoon coarse-ground black pepper
1 teaspoon kosher salt
1 tablespoon hot sauce
4 10-ounce whole Louisiana speckled or rainbow trout, dressed †
Crawfish Dressing (recipe above)
2 tablespoons extra-virgin olive oil
2 tablespoons butter
1 lemon, halved
4 large fresh dill fronds

1. Preheat oven to 350 degrees. 2. Place the flour in a shallow baking dish. 3. Mix the buttermilk, Creole mustard, cayenne, black pepper, salt and hot sauce together in a small bowl. Submerge the trout in the buttermilk mixture and marinate in the refrigerator for 10-15 minutes. Remove and drain well.
4. Use a tablespoon to gently fill the cavities of each fish with one-fourth of the crawfish dressing. Insert a skewer or toothpick across the cavity to seal the space and hold it together while cooking.
5. Gently dredge each piece of trout in flour and shake off the excess. Repeat by placing each piece back in the buttermilk mixture and again in the flour. Shake off excess. 6. To a cast-iron pan over medium heat, add the extra-virgin olive oil and butter. Place the fish in the hot pan and cook for 5 minutes on each side. 7. Finish the fish in the oven for 5 minutes, or until the trout reaches an internal temperature of 150 degrees.

*Try Zatarain's Creole mustard, available in most well-stocked grocery stores, online at zatarains.com, at Zydeco's 5 or on our Web site, zydecos.net

† Be sure to ask your local fish monger to dress the trout. They'll be happy to assist.

serves 4

fish and seafood (fruits de mer)

Distribute brussels sprouts around each plate, garnish this dish with lemon wedges and serve

blackened RED SNAPPER WITH CHIPOTLE AIOLI, TIGER SHRIMP, CREOLE SAUCE AND HAMMERED BRUSSELS SPROUTS

Julia Child said, "If you are worried about using butter, substitute with heavy cream." * This is a variation of Crab Imperial, an old-school New Orleans appetizer. * I serve it with a Creole sauce and tiny little cabbages (because I really like tiny little cabbages). Here then is a recipe for "more heavy cream in place of all the butter."

creole sauce

- ½ cup diced onion
- ¼ cup diced celery
- ½ cup diced green bell pepper
- 2 toes garlic, sliced
- ½ tablespoon salt
- ½ tablespoon black pepper
- 1 teaspoon hot sauce
- 1 tablespoon marjoram
- 2 tablespoons tomato paste
- 16 ounces whole tomatoes, in juice

1. In a medium saucepan, sauté the onion, celery, bell pepper, garlic, salt, black pepper, hot sauce and ½ tablespoon of the marjoram for 5 minutes. **2.** Add the tomato paste and continue to cook for 1 minute. Add the tomatoes, breaking them apart with a spoon. Cover and simmer over low heat for 30 minutes. **3.** Add the remaining marjoram. Remove from heat and set aside.

serves 4

shrimp sauté

- ½ cup extra-virgin olive oil
- 1 teaspoon kosher salt
- 1 teaspoon black pepper
- ½ teaspoon granulated garlic
- ½ tablespoon thyme leaves
- 1 tablespoon Worcestershire sauce
- ½ teaspoon paprika
- 1 teaspoon hot sauce
- ¼ teaspoon crab boil *
- 1 bay leaf
- 1 lemon, halved
- 1 pound raw 26-30-count tiger shrimp, peeled and deveined

1. Pour oil into a large, hot sauté pan. When it just begins to smoke, add all of the ingredients except the lemon and shrimp. Squeeze half of the lemon over the pan and drop it in; stir. **2.** Add the shrimp, stir and cook for 3-4 minutes. Reduce the heat if the pan begins to smoke too heavily or the shrimp begin to burn. **3.** Sauté until the shrimp are completely pink and just cooked through. Squeeze and add the remaining lemon. Remove shrimp and set aside. Reserve pan sauce.

red snapper

- 1 tablespoon chipotle peppers in adobo sauce
- 2 cups mayonnaise
- 4 6-8-ounce red snapper filets
- 1 tablespoon dried thyme
- 1 tablespoon paprika
- 1 teaspoon kosher salt
- 1 tablespoon black pepper
- 1 teaspoon granulated garlic
- ¼ stick butter
- 4 tablespoons olive oil
- 1 pound Shrimp Sauté (recipe above)

1. Preheat oven to 350 degrees. **2.** In a small mixing bowl, blend the chipotle peppers and mayonnaise. Set aside. **3.** Season the skin side of each snapper filet with thyme, paprika, salt, pepper and garlic. **4.** In a heavy cast-iron skillet, melt the butter and olive oil until it just begins to smoke. Place the snapper, skin side down, in the pan. Sear for 3 minutes over medium-high heat. **5.** Gently turn each filet over and spread ¼ cup of the chipotle mixture on each. Distribute the shrimp evenly over the filets. **6.** Put the skillet in the 350-degree oven for 5-7 minutes or until the fish reaches an internal temperature of 140 degrees.

hammered brussels sprouts

- 2 tablespoons butter
- 1 pound brussels sprouts
- ½ cup diced onion
- 1 teaspoon kosher salt
- 1 teaspoon black pepper
- 1 teaspoon dried thyme
- ½ teaspoon fennel seed
- 1 cup chicken stock

1. Melt the butter in a large saucepan. **2.** Add the brussels sprouts to the saucepan and allow them to brown, cooking for about 5 minutes. Turn and allow the other sides to brown, about 5 minutes. **3.** Add the onion, salt, pepper, thyme and fennel seed. Sauté for 1 minute. **4.** Add the stock and allow the mixture to simmer until most of the liquid has cooked off, about 30 minutes.

to plate

1. Onto 4 heated plates, spoon equal amounts of Creole sauce. **2.** Place the snapper on top of the sauce. **3.** Drizzle the shrimp sauté sauce over the fish.

*Try Zatarain's Concentrated Liquid Shrimp and Crab Boil, available at most well-stocked grocery stores, online at zatarains.com, at Zydeco's, or on our Web site, zydecos.net.

fish and seafood (fruits de mer)

chapter 5

Call your friends, roll out a stack of newspapers and grab a handful of fresh crawfish.

FAT TUESDAY
"MOMMY, MAKE THE SCARY WOMAN GO AWAY!"

It's Mardi Gras and this is your last chance. Put on the fishnet stockings, put on the red lipstick. Put on the low-cut red dress, the rouge, the earrings, the jewelry, the beads. And you women? You gals wear something fun, too!

"...and I'm goin' ova by my momma's for some king cake..."

It's the last time to you can cut loose! The big day in predominately Catholic locales around the world in which you see one big blowout before Ash Wednesday and Lent. Yes, Lent is a time to do without, the time to eat stale bread and drink flat, warm cola. It's when you have to wear uncomfortable shoes, sit on a tack and atone for your sins. Lent: When you give up the balloons, clowns, the flying monkeys wearing fezzes and any other kind of fun that your evil mind can imagine. Lent: A time to think of all the stupid things you've done up to this point and promise your creator that you will do better.

"You were driving erratically. Can I see some identification, sir?"

So, Tuesday (Fat) and Wednesday (Lent) are still hours away. Walk out on the balcony with your gallon of beer(s). Watch a river of bodies roll up and down Bourbon, the Krewes roll down the avenue, the marching bands thunder down Canal, Tchoupitoulas Indians strut their stuff. It's everything you've seen on those lurid cable television programs and much, much more.

"Trow me sometin' mistah!"

Actually, they will only show you a small fraction of what is really happening in the city, in south Louisiana, in and along the Gulf Coast. I don't mean that there is so much unspeakable debauchery and bacchanal excess that even cable television can't show it. Don't think that Mardi Gras is just that.

"I got some beads for ya, if..."

There are many family friendly parades. Safe, calm and just as much fun. They will actually stop the parade so that your kid can get a little prize. I have been lucky enough to be in some of those parades, giving out beads to moms and dads and their kids. I must say, it was a blast.

"I know where you got your shoes."

There are elegant parties that require tux and tails. There are dances and concerts and art events and beautiful open houses to visit. I guess the TV producers think they can only show the more lurid and titillating aspects of the festivities. The cool, elegant, sophisticated and mature stuff is, to me, some of the best stuff we have to offer. That must be bad for the ratings, so you will never see any of it.

"Laissez les bon temps roulez, ya'll!"

But hey, I like to have fun as much as the next guy. Just come in to Zydeco's. You'll see we have almost every nook and cranny filled with thousands of pictures of us having a good time. Here is a little treasure

hunt for you, a little gift from me to you. Look for a picture of a crazy ugly lady in a red dress, five o'clock shadow, a cigar in one hand and a shot of whisky in the other.

"Mommy, make the scary woman go away!"

When the picture was taken, she was singing to the karaoke version of "I am Woman" in a croaky voice. I'll say nothing else on the subject other than I had laryngitis for a week, probably from all of those cigars and whisky.

"No Public Bathroom, Don't Ask."

Another way I love to celebrate is to indulge in great food. Every town has very specific things they like to serve on Fat Tuesday and there are recipes that are, if not ubiquitous, outright cliché. They are all still fun to make and eat, so you won't see me complain. The recipes in this chapter meet the Mardi Gras criteria: Fun to make and fun to eat (and I think you will enjoy them more than hearing me sing).

"I got two Schwegmann bags full of beads, what you got?"

Taking part in a crawfish boil at Zydeco's 5 in Mooresville, Indiana, Jerome and Terrebonne aren't shy about beheading the black-eyed, fire-red entrée

Line a community table with newspaper and dump the crawfish out to serve.

crawfish boil
(L'ECREVISSE BOUILLE)

The first time I boiled crawfish, I was a very young boy, crouching behind my house in Paradis, Louisiana. My setup was a coffee can filled halfway with water sitting over a little fire, and the boil consisted of one crawfish I caught with the help of my collie. Today, during their season in the spring I boil sacks and sacks of crawfish for the customers at Zydeco's. As good as they are, it still doesn't match my memories of that first intimate boil with my dog all those years ago.

- 12 lemons, halved
- 3 oranges, halved
- 1½ cups liquid crab boil *
- 4 cups kosher salt
- 2 cups black pepper
- 2 cups cayenne
- 1 bottle hot sauce, or to taste
- 3 onions, halved
- 3 green bell peppers, seeded and halved
- 3 bay leaves
- 1 bunch celery, stalks halved
- 12 toes garlic, halved
- 1 35-pound sack live crawfish, cleaned +
- 24 half-ears corn on the cob
- 12 small red potatoes, boiled

1. You will need a large crawfish pot with a burner or a large turkey fryer. Fill the pot with 9 inches of water. Put all ingredients, except crawfish, corn on the cob and potatoes, into the crawfish pot; cover. Bring to a boil and cook for 30 minutes. 2. Add crawfish, cover and cook for 15 minutes. Turn off the heat, stir and add the corn on the cob and potatoes. Let the boil soak for 30 minutes to 1 hour. The longer the soak, the spicier the end result.

*Try Zatarain's Concentrated Liquid Shrimp and Crab Boil, available at most well-stocked grocery stores, online at zatarains.com, at Zydeco's 5 or on our Web site, zydecos.net

+You can purchase live crawfish online from multiple Louisiana crawfish farms. They will be shipped, live, overnight. Hutch recommends Kyle LeBlanc Crawfish Farms, crawdads.net; The Louisiana Crawfish Company, lacrawfish.com; or The Louisiana Cajun Crawfish Company, crawfishcoofcentralflain.com. You can also buy crawfish at Zydeco's 5 or online at zydecos.net. Live blue Louisiana crabs can be used as well with good results, as can head-on shrimp. Cooking time would be 5 minutes instead of 15 for the shrimp, or 8 for the crab.

serves 8-12

Serve immediately with a side of hot fresh French bread to dip in the butter sauce

les chevrettes
BOUCANÉ BOUTTE
(BBQ SHRIMP)

New Orleans always does things a little differently than the rest of the country. It's true we follow the beat of our own jazzy drummer. BBQ shrimp in New Orleans is the process of sautéing shrimp in butter and spices, and has nothing at all to do with the grill, a pitmaster or a tangy, bottled sauce. BBQ shrimp is always a big hit at the Z, and I think you'll agree, it's an easy, flavorful way to dress your shrimp.

serves 8

- 2 pounds butter (yes, 2 pounds)
- 2 tablespoons kosher salt
- 2 tablespoons black pepper
- 2 tablespoons red pepper flakes
- 1 tablespoon paprika
- 2 tablespoons thyme leaves
- 2 tablespoons cayenne powder
- 1 tablespoon granulated garlic
- 4 tablespoons Worcestershire sauce
- 4 tablespoons Tabasco brand hot sauce
- ½ cup chopped green onion
- 1 teaspoon red pepper flakes
- 1 tablespoon Zatarain's Concentrated Liquid Shrimp and Crab Boil *
- 2 lemons, halved
- 4 pounds, 8-12-count raw shrimp, shells on
- 8 ounces prepared Tasso (recipe on page 31), cut into ¼-inch strips
- French bread, to serve

1. Put all ingredients except the shrimp, tasso and 1 lemon (2 halves) into a large sauté pan. Cook over high heat for 1 minute, stirring continuously. **2.** Add the shrimp, cover and cook on high until shrimp turn pink and are just cooked through, about 3-5 minutes. **3.** Remove lid, add tasso and cook for 1 minute. Squeeze the remaining lemon over the shrimp. **4.** Place the finished shrimp and sauce on a large serving platter.

* Zatarain's is available at most well-stocked grocery stores, online at zatarains.com, at Zydeco's 5 or on our Web site, zydecos.net

Slice the crab, artichoke and garlic pizza and serve

crab, artichoke AND GARLIC PIZZA

I used to get a pizza much like this at a little place in Covington, Louisiana. It was made by a man behind a large plate-glass window. He would deftly toss the pizza dough high into the air. The flying disks would expand then swirl back to earth. Since he used fresh Louisiana crabmeat, the final result was nothing short of amazing. Simple, hot and delicious. ✻ Then, many years later, while in Bari, Italy, could it be? There it was; a crab and artichoke pizza. It was made by a man who deftly tossed the pizza dough high into the air. It was great because of its simplicity and use of local Puglian ingredients. Two men, thousands of miles apart, both understanding their food. Artists making something wonderful. Loads of fresh crabmeat, artichoke hearts, garlic and extra-virgin olive oil make this a nice change of pace from the ordinary. The beauty is in its simplicity.

yeast starter

- 1¼ cups all-purpose flour
- 1 tablespoon fast-acting yeast
- Pinch kosher salt
- 2 tablespoons extra-virgin olive oil
- 2½ cups water, 110 degrees

1. In a large, stainless-steel bowl, combine all of the ingredients. **2.** Cover with a kitchen towel and put in a draft-free, warm place for 15 minutes. (The mixture should be bubbling.)

dough*

- 2½ cups all-purpose flour, plus more to flour work surface
- Yeast Starter (recipe above)
- 1 tablespoon olive oil

1. Add the flour, 1 cup at a time, to the yeast starter and mix well. (The dough should be slightly sticky and very soft.) **2.** Turn the mix out onto a floured surface and knead the dough for 10 minutes. Cut into 2 equal parts. Wrap 1 and freeze for later use. **3.** Place the oil in a large mixing bowl. Place the dough in the bowl and turn, lightly coating the outside of the dough with oil. **4.** Allow the dough to rise at room temperature for 1 hour or until it has doubled in size. **5.** On a lightly floured surface, roll the dough out to the desired crust thickness.

topping

- 1 uncooked crust (Dough recipe above)
- 1 pound real crabmeat
- 2 15-ounce cans artichoke hearts in water, 6-8-count, drained and sliced
- 8 toes garlic, thinly sliced
- 1 tablespoon kosher salt
- 1 tablespoon black pepper
- Extra-virgin olive oil, as needed

1. Preheat oven to 450 degrees. **2.** Top the rolled-out pizza dough with the lump crabmeat, artichoke hearts, garlic, kosher salt and pepper and drizzle heavily with extra-virgin olive oil. **3.** Bake the pizza in the 450-degree oven for 20-30 minutes or until the crust is crispy and light brown.

*This dough recipe yields enough for 2 pizza crusts

makes 1 large pizza

Sprinkle liberally with beignet seasoning and serve with a drizzle of soy sauce

beignet l'ecrevisse

For most people, the word "beignet" conjures up images of the French Quarter doughnut, piled high with mounds of powdered sugar. You might be surprised to learn that New Orleans natives serve up savory beignets as well. In a stroke of genius, someone dropped the sugar and added copious amounts of sautéed vegetables, seafood, meats and poultry to beignet dough. It is then scooped out by the spoonful, deep-fried in peanut oil and covered with savory beignet seasonings. It's old-school "Nouvelle Orleans". This is my recipe for the wildly popular savory crawfish beignet I serve at The Z.

savory beignet seasoning

- 2 tablespoons paprika
- 2 tablespoons granulated garlic
- 2 tablespoons dried parsley flakes
- 4 tablespoons kosher salt
- 6 tablespoons black pepper
- 6 tablespoons thyme leaves

1. Combine ingredients and set aside.

beignets

- 2 cups diced onions
- 2 cups diced green, red and yellow bell peppers
- 4 tablespoons extra-virgin olive oil
- 1 teaspoon plus 1 pinch kosher salt
- 1 teaspoon black pepper
- 1 teaspoon thyme leaves
- Pinch cayenne
- 1 toe garlic, minced
- 6 cups flour
- 2 packets instant-dry yeast
- 3 cups water, 100 degrees
- 1 pound crawfish tail meat, chopped
- 2 quarts peanut oil
- Beignet Seasoning (recipe above), as needed
- Soy sauce, as needed

1. In a medium sauté pan, sauté the onions and bell peppers in 3 tablespoons extra-virgin olive oil. 2. Add 1 teaspoon kosher salt, black pepper, thyme, cayenne and garlic. Cook until the onions are translucent, about 10 minutes. Set aside to cool. 3. In a large mixing bowl, combine 3 cups flour with the yeast, pinch of kosher salt, 1 tablespoon extra-virgin olive oil and water. Cover with aluminum foil or plastic wrap and proof for 15-20 minutes. The mixture should be frothy, indicating that the yeast is active. 4. Stir in the sautéed onions, bell peppers and crawfish. 5. Gradually incorporate the 3 cups of flour into the dough, mixing with your hands to make a soft and slightly sticky dough. 6. Cover with aluminum foil or plastic wrap, refrigerate and allow the dough to rise until it has doubled in size, about 2-3 hours. 7. In a 4-quart stockpot, heat the peanut oil to 365 degrees. 8. Using a large spoon, scoop 2-3-ounce balls of the beignet dough out onto a floured surface. Sprinkle the top with flour and flatten the dough by pressing down gently with the palm of your hand. 9. Carefully drop the balls, in batches, into the peanut oil and fry for 2-3 minutes per side, or until they are cooked through and golden brown. Drain the beignets on paper towels.

makes about 2 dozen beignets

Splash with hot sauce, ketchup, salt and lemon juice to taste and close the sandwich

Cut the sandwich into quarters and plate with a generous helping of gaufrettes (waffle chips).

muffulettas
WITH GAUFRETTES

As a restaurant owner, when I see a busload of people lined up around the block waiting for an hour to get a sandwich, a little voice begins to whisper softly to me. When said restaurant owner is also in line with other expectant patrons, that muse of inspiration, let's call her "Loretta", begins to stroke my ego and goad me on to try to replicate that success. ✳ *"Hey, baby, you could do this in Indiana!"* ✳ "Naw, it seems too simple." ✳ *"It's a great sandwich and you love it, don't you?"* ✳ "Yeah, it's a good thing, a great sandwich and I do love it. Look at me standing in line with all of these people. Do you really think I can do it at my restaurant?" ✳ *"All of these people can't be wrong. You can do this; you will sell billions of 'em!"*

serves 8

So, back at Zydeco's and with the nudging of Loretta, I made the special muffuletta bread (because you can't just pop into the local market and pick it up). I made the olive dressing (because the megastores just don't carry it).

"Come on, Loretta, this is a lot of work. Is it worth it?"

"Yeah, baby. Do it for me, do it for us. I know you want to. Remember all those people back home clamoring for it; waiting in line for it? Imagine all of the people here that will clamor for it, clamor for you!"

"OK baby, let's do it."

I used tons of ham, genoa salami, mortadella, Swiss and provolone, because I wanted my muffuletta to have more flavor, more of everything; to be better than the original. That, and Loretta was making all kinds of promises to me, wild success, fame, fortune, possibly the Nobel Prize. And she's right. It's a great sandwich, a New Orleans tradition and I had successfully conjured them up in the Midwest. Stand back Indiana, here comes my muffuletta, so get ready for greatness…

…and the people stayed away in droves.

One restaurant critic said it was a good sandwich, but she didn't like olives. Wow, just meat, cheese and bread. Boy, did she not get it. Others asked for mayonnaise or ketchup. What? Some wanted it on a hamburger bun or just sliced bread. I worked for hours making really good homemade bread. When I explained the sandwich to them—the history, the place it holds in the hearts and minds of New Orleanians—some looked like deer caught in headlights. Could I have been so wrong? And where was Loretta, anyway?

I couldn't give them away. Of course, New Orleans natives and ex-pats couldn't believe their luck in finding a damn good Muff in the Midwest, but I wanted more than that. Were there lines around the block, fame and fortune, a nomination for president? No. Loretta and I both ran up against the cultural divide. Pockets of local culture that, when transplanted to another area, may prove difficult to take root. But I knew that if the people just tried one, they would understand.

Ten years and many false starts later, the muffuletta is slowly making its way into the collective conscience of my customers. A small part of Louisiana culture is taking hold and beginning to grow in the Midwest, and that's a good thing.

Loretta and I are friends once more. When I am in line at that little shop on Decatur Street, waiting an hour for a muffuletta, she whispers sweet nothings into my ear and we plan the next "big thing" at Zydeco's. It's gonna be great.

p.s. Loretta told me to put this recipe in the cookbook because it will make me rich and famous. She told me to tell you that you should make this for your next party. I have to agree with her, it really is a great sandwich and your friends will love it. Come on, she knows you want to.

muffuletta olive dressing

- 5½ cups Manzanilla olives
- 2 cups kalamata olives
- 4 cups pickled cauliflower
- 1 cup pepperoncinis, sliced
- 1 cup carrots, thinly sliced
- 1 stalk celery, thinly sliced
- 1 cup cocktail onions
- 2 tablespoons capers
- 1 tablespoon celery seed
- 1 tablespoon dried basil leaves
- 1 tablespoon marjoram
- 1 tablespoon black pepper
- 1 teaspoon salt
- 1 teaspoon granulated garlic

1. In a large bowl, use a fork to lightly crush the Manzanilla and kalamata olives.
2. Add the remaining ingredients and gently mix.
3. Transfer the dressing to clean canning jars. Store in the refrigerator until needed.

Yields 1 gallon

(recipe continued on page 94)

(recipe continued from page 93)

muffuletta bread

YEAST
1¼ cups bread flour
1 tablespoon fast-acting yeast
Pinch kosher salt
2 tablespoons extra-virgin olive oil
2½ cups water, 110 degrees

1. For the yeast, in a large stainless-steel bowl, mix all of the ingredients. Cover and place in a draft-free warm spot for 15 minutes. **2.** At the end of 15 minutes, the mixture should be bubbling.

DOUGH
2½ cups bread flour, plus more as needed
Yeast (recipe above)
1 tablespoon olive oil, plus more as needed
3 tablespoons sesame seeds
1 egg
1 tablespoon water

1. For the dough, preheat oven to 375 degrees. **2.** Add the flour to the prepared yeast starter and mix well. **3.** Turn the dough out onto a floured work surface and knead for 10 minutes. **4.** Place 1 tablespoon of olive oil in a large bowl. Add the dough and turn, lightly covering the dough in oil. Allow the dough to rise for 1 hour. **5.** Cut the dough into 3 equal portions, each about 18 ounces, or the size of a softball. **6.** Form each portion into a ball and lightly coat in olive oil. Place each ball into a lightly floured 9-inch non-stick pie pan. Press down on the top of the dough with your palm to flatten into a disk shape. Sprinkle sesame seeds on top of each loaf. Let the dough rise for 1 hour in a draft-free warm place. **7.** Mix the egg and water to make an egg wash. Brush the egg wash on top of each loaf. **8.** Bake in the 375-degree oven for 45 minutes.

sandwich

Muffuletta loaves (recipe above)
1 pound sliced ham
1 pound sliced mortadella
1 pound sliced genoa salami
1 pound sliced Swiss cheese
1 pound sliced provolone
Muffuletta Olive Dressing (recipe on page 93)

1. Cut the muffuletta loaves in half horizontally to make 2 disks (6 disks total). **2.** Place an equal amount of meat and cheese slices on the bottom half of each loaf. Top with a generous portion of the olive dressing. Finish with the top of the bread. **3.** Cover the sandwich with wax paper. Press down on the sandwich, and place a heavy pan or weight on top. Let the completed sandwich rest for 30 minutes.

gaufrettes (waffle chips)

2 large sweet potatoes
2 quarts peanut oil
2 tablespoons kosher salt
4 tablespoons brown sugar
1 teaspoon cayenne

1. Wash the sweet potatoes, but do not peel. Slice the sweet potatoes using the waffle blade on your mandolin. Turn the potatoes 90 degrees on every pass to create a lattice pattern on the slices. **2.** Soak in cool water for about 1 hour, replacing with fresh water three or four times to remove excess starch. Remove the potatoes and pat dry. **3.** Place 2 quarts of peanut oil in a 4-quart pot. Heat the oil to 350 degrees. **4.** Drop the waffle chips into the oil and fry until crisp and golden brown, about 2-3 minutes. Remove and drain on paper towels. **5.** Sprinkle with salt, sugar and cayenne. Serve immediately with fresh muffulettas.

peacemakers WITH HORSERADISH AIOLI

You just stayed out all night drinking with the boys and your wife is less than pleased. You splurged on a pricey pair of leather heels and your husband doesn't share your passion for fashion. You forgot to pick up your kids at school. (You remember them, right?) For all of these reasons and many, many more, I share with you The Peacemaker. ✶ If you were back in New Orleans and made this sandwich, your significant other would wonder why you felt so guilty, as this meal is traditionally made as an act of contrition. It got its name for its ability to ameliorate, or soothe the rough spots and make them better. It's the dry wall patch, the sugar in the medicine, the dozen red roses, the olive branch, a fried-seafood-and-carbohydrate prayer of forgiveness. ✶ Personally, I think The Peacemaker is just a great sandwich, regardless of what you plan to get into.

- 2 quarts vegetable oil
- 1 cup mayonnaise
- 1 tablespoon grated horseradish
- 1 loaf French bread, halved lengthwise
- 3 cups flour
- 6 eggs, whisked
- 3 cups bread crumbs
- 1 tablespoon dried thyme leaves
- ½ tablespoon marjoram
- ½ tablespoon dried basil
- ½ tablespoon black pepper
- ½ tablespoon granulated garlic
- 1 tablespoon hot sauce, plus more to taste
- 1 pound 26-30-count shrimp, peeled and deveined, tails on
- ½ pound fresh gulf oysters, shucked
- Ketchup, to taste
- Kosher salt, to taste
- Lemon juice, to taste

1. Place the oil in a 4-quart stockpot and heat to 350 degrees. **2.** In a medium mixing bowl, combine the mayonnaise and horseradish. Spread the mixture over both sides of the sliced French bread. **3.** Using 3 small trays or shallow bowls, make a fry station. On the first tray, put the flour. In the second tray, place the whisked eggs. In the third tray, place the bread crumbs. Mix the thyme, marjoram, basil, pepper and garlic in with the bread crumbs. Mix 1 tablespoon of hot sauce in with the eggs. **4.** Bread the shrimp and oysters by dredging them first in the flour, then the eggs, then the bread crumbs. **5.** Fry the shrimp in the heated oil for 2-3 minutes or until they achieve a golden-brown crust. Fry the oysters for 1 minute. Remove with a slotted spoon and drain on paper towels. **6.** To serve, pile the fried shrimp and oysters high on the French bread.

(pictured on page 90)

serves 4 (or 1 if you were really bad)

Sprinkle with chopped parsley and serve with pickled mirliton spears and Creole cream cheese.

buffaleaux wings
WITH CREOLE CREAM CHEESE AND PICKLED MIRLITON

As the faux spelling implies, this is a Cajun version of the ubiquitous chicken finger food. In New Orleans, we can party with the best of them and of course, we had to put our own spin on it. Buffaleaux wings are my variation of a classic étouffée, suitably rich, flavorful and spicy. When I give cooking demonstrations, I pull out this recipe and everybody just loves it. You can use this method on turkey wings, too, making a fantastic dish that is often served in and around Thibodaux. I think it would make a great dish at your next party.

serves 4-8

refrigerator pickled mirliton

- 1 mirliton
- 1¼ cups vinegar
- 1 teaspoon mustard seed
- 1 teaspoon black peppercorns
- 1 teaspoon sugar
- 2 toes garlic, crushed
- 1 whole cayenne pepper
- 1 bay leaf

1. Wash a blemish-free mirliton under cool water and dry. Peel and cut the vegetable first into thirds lengthwise, and then each third into ½-inch sticks. **2.** In a medium stainless-steel bowl, combine all of the ingredients except the mirliton. **3.** Place the mirliton slices in a widemouthed pint jar. Pour the pickling liquid over the mirliton. Secure the jar lid and refrigerate the mirliton for 3 days prior to serving.

creole cream cheese*

- 1 gallon skim milk
- 2 cups cultured buttermilk
- 5 drops vegetable rennet †

1. In a stainless-steel pot, combine the skim milk and buttermilk. **2.** Insert an instant-read thermometer and bring the milk mixture to 90 degrees, stirring occasionally and gently. **3.** Remove the pot from the heat and add the vegetable rennet. Stir gently. **4.** Allow a curd to form by leaving the pot covered with a warm towel or in the oven (not turned on) for 12 hours. **5.** Pour the contents through a large sieve to drain the whey. Refrigerate and allow the mixture to continue draining through the sieve for 8 hours. **6.** Pack the cream cheese in clean containers.

brine

- ½ cup kosher salt
- ½ cup sugar
- 1 gallon cold water

1. Combine the brine ingredients and set aside.

buffaleaux wings

- 5 pounds chicken wings (first and second wing joints)
- Brine (recipe above)
- 4 tablespoons extra-virgin olive oil
- 1 cup diced onions
- ½ cup diced celery
- 1 cup diced red, yellow and green bell peppers
- 2 tablespoons tomato paste
- 1 cup white wine
- 1 tablespoon dried thyme leaves
- 1 tablespoon black pepper
- 1 tablespoon cayenne
- 1 tablespoon salt
- ½ tablespoon red pepper flakes
- 1 tablespoon paprika
- 1 bay leaf
- 4 tablespoons hot sauce, plus more to garnish
- 6 toes garlic, sliced
- 1 cup chicken stock
- 1 tablespoon flour
- ¼ cup chopped fresh parsley

1. Submerge the wings in the brine solution and soak for 2-4 hours. Drain, rinse and pat the wings dry. **2.** In a large cast-iron pan, heat the olive oil until lightly smoking. (Careful not to burn the oil.) **3.** When the oil is hot, brown the wings, in batches so as not to overcrowd the pan, for 5 minutes on each side. Remove and set aside. **4.** To the hot pan, add the onions, celery and bell peppers. Sauté for 1 minute, scraping the bottom of the pan. **5.** Add the tomato paste and sauté for 2 minutes. **6.** Add the wine and sauté for 1 minute. **7.** Transfer all of the wings back into the pan. Add the thyme, black pepper, cayenne, salt, red pepper flakes, paprika, bay leaf, hot sauce and garlic. Sauté for 1 minute. **8.** Add the chicken stock and bring the heat up so the contents are at a high simmer. **9.** Reduce the heat to low and cook the wings at a low simmer for 15 minutes. **10.** Lightly sprinkle the flour over the top of the wings. Cover and cook for an additional 5 minutes. **11.** Gently stir the wings. Place on a large serving platter.

*This recipe yields 2 pounds of Creole cream cheese

†You can purchase vegetable rennet at Zydeco's 5, on our Web site, zydecos.net, or you can find a simple recipe and make your own.

Serve the oreilles sales with a dollop of sour cream, soy sauce and/or savory Creole cream cheese.

oreilles sales
(PIGS EARS 3 WAYS)

Often times, upon first mentioning this recipe, people think I am cooking up real pig ears. But as I always explain, the title actually refers to the shape and texture of the fried pastry. While these are usually served as a sweet dessert, I have transformed them into a savory dish with the addition of boudin, oysters and shrimp.

oreilles sales (pig ears)

- 1 green onion
- 1 egg
- ½ cup water
- 2 cups all-purpose flour
- 2 teaspoons baking powder
- Pinch salt

1. Cut the green onion into 12 long, thin strips. 2. In a medium mixing bowl, use a whisk to combine the egg and water. 3. In a separate medium mixing bowl, sift together the flour, baking powder and salt. 4. Slowly add the dry ingredients to the water/egg mixture and use a spoon or your hands to blend until a soft dough forms. 5. Shape into 12 small, 1-ounce balls. Roll the "ears" out on a lightly floured cutting board or work surface until very thin, about 1/8-inch thick.

makes 12 ears

boudin and creole mustard

- ½ pound Boudin (recipe on page 25), casing removed
- 4 teaspoons Creole mustard *

1. Divide the boudin into 4 equal portions and place on top of 4 prepared, rolled out oreilles sales. 2. Top each with 1 teaspoon of Creole mustard. 3. Pull up the edges to form a sack (similar to a peasant's bag) and tie a strip of green onion around the top to hold. Set aside until ready for frying.

makes enough filling for 4 ears

shrimp, tomato and basil

- ½ pound sautéed 26-30-count shrimp
- 1 small Creole tomato +, seeded and chopped
- 4 leaves fresh basil

1. Divide the shrimp, tomato and basil into 4 equal portions. Place a portion on top of each of 4 rolled out oreilles sales. 2. Pull up the edges to form a sack (similar to a peasant's bag) and tie around the top with a strip of green onion to hold. Set aside until ready for frying.

makes enough filling for 4 ears

oyster, artichoke and bacon

- 4 canned artichoke bottoms, drained
- 4 fresh gulf oysters, shucked
- 4 slices cooked bacon, diced

1. On each of the 4 remaining oreilles sales, place an artichoke bottom, one portion of oyster meat and one portion of diced bacon. 2. Pull up the edges to form a sack (similar to a peasant's bag) and tie around the top with a strip of green onion to hold. Set aside until ready for frying.

makes enough filling for 4 ears

To assemble

Vegetable oil, for deep-frying
Kosher salt, to taste
Sour cream, to serve
Soy sauce, to serve,
Creole Cream Cheese (recipe on page 97), to serve

1. In a large pot or deep fryer, preheat the vegetable oil to 350 degrees. Fry all oreilles sales, in batches if necessary, for 3-4 minutes or until golden brown. 2. Using a slotted spoon, remove the sacks from the oil and drain on paper towels. Sprinkle with kosher salt.

*Look for Zatarain's Creole mustard in well-stocked grocery stores, online at zatarains.com, at Zydeco's 5 or on our Web site zydecos.net.

+Creole tomatoes are medium-size tomatoes developed to survive the warm and humid climate of the south. They are very popular in south Louisiana, but if they don't stock them at your local farmers market, use any fresh, local tomato.

serves 4

*Your friends can supply the music, sirens and debauchery.

duck and andouille JAMBALAYA

I was fortunate to live for a time just outside Baton Rouge in Gonzales, Louisiana, the official "Jambalaya Capitol of the World." Jambalaya is a social food. It's usually made for the big event, the music festival, the end of the marathon, the fais do-do, the intermission at the concert, for you and your closest eleventy-billion friends. Jambalaya is almost always made in big batches, with stupidly large cast-iron pots, with tons of meats and rice and gallons of stock, stirred with boat paddles over crackling wooden fires that are on the verge of setting the place ablaze. Steam and smoke and loud noises and music and sirens and debauchery are almost always associated with jambalaya, at least the good batches. * It's the number one seller at The Z5. I make gallon upon gallon of the stuff every week and yet, I always seem to run out. I have made large crawfish pots of jambalaya at huge events in Indianapolis and in the parking lot for the little town parade. I have shown it on Indianapolis TV and served buckets of it at private parties. Some nights, I make the stuff in my dreams. * Jambalaya is a bit tricky to master. It's your first bike. It's your first time behind the wheel, grinding the gears of a manual transmission. It's old school. It has a million souls behind it and over two centuries of history in it and it will try to spank you. Don't let it boss you around. It takes a little practice to know when you are cooking it too fast or too slow. Too fast, and it's scorched. Too slow and it turns to a big blob of starch. How many times have I messed up a jambalaya? More times than I care to mention. Don't be discouraged, you can do this. The best advice I can give you is to practice, practice, practice. It's worth the time and effort.

- 3 pounds boneless duck thighs, 1-inch dice
- 4 tablespoons extra-virgin olive oil
- 3 pounds Andouille sausage (recipe on page 23), sliced into rounds
- 4 tablespoons browning sauce
- 4 tablespoons Worcestershire sauce
- ½ tablespoon liquid smoke
- 2 cups large-dice onions
- 1 cup medium-dice celery
- 3 cups large-dice red, yellow and green bell peppers
- ½ tablespoon cayenne powder
- 6 toes garlic, sliced
- 1 tablespoon fresh thyme
- 1 tablespoon black pepper
- 1 bay leaf
- ¼ cup white wine
- 6 quarts duck or chicken stock
- 6 tablespoons chicken base
- 6 cups rice

1. In a large, 15-quart pot over high heat, brown the duck in olive oil. Add the sausage, browning sauce, Worcestershire and liquid smoke. Cook for 1 minute. Add the onions, celery, bell peppers, cayenne powder, garlic, thyme, black pepper and bay leaf and cook for an additional 5 minutes. Add the wine and cook for 1 minute.
2. Add the stock and chicken base and bring the mixture to a boil. Let the mixture boil just until heated through.
3. Remove and discard the bay leaf. Add rice; stir, cover and cook for 1 minute.
4. Scrape the crispy rice from the bottom and mix in with the rest of the rice, reduce the heat to medium and cover. At this point, the jambalaya should be at a strong simmer. Cook for 5 minutes.
5. Scrape the rice from the bottom, replace lid and reduce heat to medium-low. The jambalaya should now be at a low simmer.
6. Stir the jambalaya every 5 minutes, scraping from the bottom. Cook for 40 minutes or until the rice is tender and moist but not soaking in liquid. *

serves 18-20

chapter 6

PASTA (PÂTES)
RED BEAN MONDAYS, MEATLESS FRIDAYS AND SPAGHETTI WEDNESDAYS

I always feel a certain amount of accomplishment when I can sneak a few more pasta dishes onto the Zydeco's menu. To me, it's a big part of Louisiana cuisine. Any man or woman, boy or girl who is or who was a product of the southern-most Louisiana school systems will probably know this basic lunch menu:

Monday - Red Beans and Rice with Sausage

Friday - Seafood, Fried or Broiled, Catfish or Shrimps with Fries

Tuesday and Thursdays - A combination or variation of Monday and Friday

What about Wednesdays? On those days, it was invariably pasta or some other Italian-inspired dish. Why pasta? Perhaps a small part of that answer lies in the influx of Italian and Sicilian immigrants to south Louisiana. They toiled at the New Orleans port, set up businesses, worked in the fields and worked hard. They became so entrenched in the city that during a time, the French Quarter wasn't so much French or Spanish, but Italian. This led to the title "Little Italy" or "Little Sicily". The "French Market" was "The Italian Market" and so on. The influence is unmistakable. You can see it in the muffuletta sandwich from Central Grocery, crawfish and pasta at the Jazz Fest, St. Joseph's Day on March 19 with magnificent food draped altars and The Piazza D'ltalia, it's all there.

If you have read the other introductions in this book, you may ask yourself if there is some whacky pasta-inspired story I can convey. Maybe something like, "...angry hordes of Sicilians streaming through my backyard, tearing up everything and then majestically sweeping in waves and wide arcs into the swamp." Sorry, nothing so surreal. Instead, I will tell you that I have serious respect for, and have been fortunate enough to eat some, amazing Italian food. If you ever get the chance, you must visit the city for St. Joseph's Night festivities.

You may or may not know that I have traveled across just about every part of Italy, had great food and stayed with some fantastic families. I have had the distinct pleasure of being allowed into their kitchens and along the way, managed to pick up a few techniques. I could see, especially in the Puglian region in south Italy, a way of cooking and use of ingredients that exists in south Louisiana. There is a link, a method that spans the Atlantic, and there is no doubt about that. The Italian immigrants who came to the city in the 1800s and 1900s had brought with them their recipes and techniques and I was witness in some small way to the genesis of that influence.

In those Italian homes in which I stayed, I could see the connection. Hence my infatuation with south Louisiana pasta dishes. It's the love and respect of a great culture that influences the city and that influences me to this day.

Squeeze the lemon juice over the crab cakes and top with fresh parsley. Serve immediately.

blackened CRAB CAKES IN A NEST

If there is an element that runs through all of the culinary traditions of south Louisiana, it would be the layering of flavor upon flavor. Here is a wonderful dish that combines a rich, white roux-based cream sauce fortified with diced ham, shrimp and lump crabmeat, with blackened crab cakes in a nest of fettuccine.

serves 4-8

pasta

- 4 quarts water
- 2 tablespoons kosher salt
- 1 pound fettuccine noodles
- 2 tablespoons melted butter

1. In a large stockpot, bring the water to a boil. Add the salt. Cook the pasta for 12-14 minutes or until just cooked through (al dente). **2.** Drain the pasta and finish with the melted butter. Set aside.

cream sauce

- 1 stick butter
- ⅓ cup flour
- 1 leek, chopped
- 1 tablespoon thyme leaves
- 1 teaspoon kosher salt
- 1 teaspoon black pepper
- 3 toes garlic, minced
- ½ pound gumbo shrimp, uncooked
- ¼ cup chopped green onion
- ½ cup chopped fresh parsley
- ½ cup diced ham
- 2 pints heavy cream
- 1 tablespoon Worcestershire sauce
- ¼ cup white wine
- ½ pound lump crabmeat

1. In a medium saucepan, melt the butter. Slowly whisk in the flour. Cook for about 3 minutes, whisking continuously. **2.** Add the leek, thyme, salt, pepper and garlic and cook for 1 minute. **3.** Add the shrimp, green onion, parsley and ham and cook for 1 minute. **4.** Slowly add the heavy cream, Worcestershire sauce and wine and simmer for 10 minutes. **5.** Remove the pan from the heat and fold in the crabmeat. Let the sauce rest for 5 minutes.

blackened crab cakes

- 1 tablespoon Worcestershire sauce
- ½ tablespoon mayonnaise
- ½ teaspoon Creole mustard *
- ½ teaspoon kosher salt
- 3 tablespoons thyme leaves
- ½ teaspoon plus 2 tablespoons black pepper
- ¼ teaspoon Zatarain's Concentrated Crab & Shrimp Boil *
- ¾ cup chopped fresh parsley
- 2 egg whites
- 1 pound lump crabmeat
- 1 cup fresh, soft bread crumbs (do not use dry bread crumbs)
- 2 tablespoons paprika
- ½ stick butter
- 1 lemon, halved

1. In a large mixing bowl, combine the Worcestershire sauce, mayonnaise, Creole mustard, salt, 1 tablespoon thyme, ½ teaspoon black pepper, crab boil, ¼ cup parsley and egg whites. Gently fold in the crabmeat and bread crumbs. **2.** Divide the mixture into 4-8 balls and form into cakes or patties. **3.** In a shallow dish, combine the remaining 2 tablespoons thyme, 2 tablespoons black pepper and paprika to make a blackening seasoning. **4.** Coat one side of each of the crab cakes with the blackening seasoning. **5.** In a large sauté pan over medium-high heat, melt the butter. Add the crab cakes to the pan and sauté until a dark brown crust forms, about 3-4 minutes on each side. Be careful not to burn the cakes. Reduce the heat if the butter smokes excessively. **6.** To serve, divide equal amounts of pasta among 4-8 serving plates. Place a crab cake on top of the pasta. Pour the cream sauce over and around the crab cakes and pasta.

*Find Zatarain's brand crab boil and Creole mustard at most well-stocked grocery stores, online at zatarains.com, at Zydeco's 5 or on our Web site, zydecos.net

pasta (pâtes)

Plate the pasta and garnish by topping with chopped green onion and grated Asiago.

north shore
DUCK AND TASSO PASTA

I have had countless variations of this dish, with each restaurant or cook producing their own version. What makes this pasta so unique is the use of beef stock in lieu of a more traditional cream or tomato sauce. It pairs well with the heartiness of the duck and the bite of the tasso, which both complement the shape of the mezze penne pasta.

serves 4-8

pasta

- 4 quarts water
- 2 tablespoons kosher salt
- 1 pound mezze penne pasta
- 2 tablespoons unsalted, melted butter

1. In a large stockpot, bring the water to a boil. Add the salt. **2.** Cook the pasta for 12-14 minutes or until just cooked through (al dente). **3.** Drain the pasta and finish by combining it with the butter. Set aside.

Thickened beef stock

- Water, as needed
- Cornstarch as needed
- Beef stock, as needed

1. In a small mixing bowl, add water to cornstarch to make a slurry that has the consistency of heavy cream. **2.** In a small saucepot, bring the beef stock to a rolling boil. **3.** Slowly whisk in the cornstarch slurry, a little at a time, adding just enough to thicken.

duck and tasso

- 4 tablespoons unsalted butter
- 4 tablespoons extra-virgin olive oil
- 16 ounces duck confit, thighs and legs, deboned, cut into strips
- 8 ounces Pork Tasso (recipe on page 31), cut into strips
- 1 teaspoon fresh-cracked black pepper
- 1 tablespoon thyme leaves
- 3 toes garlic, thinly sliced
- 1 pound Pasta (recipe above)
- 4 cups demiglace or Thickened Beef Stock (recipe above)
- ½ cup chopped green onion
- ½ cup grated Asiago cheese

1. In a large sauté pan, melt the butter. **2.** Add the olive oil and cook until lightly smoking. **3.** Add the duck, tasso, black pepper, thyme and garlic and heat through, about 3 minutes. **4.** Add the cooked penne and sauté for about 30 seconds. **5.** Add enough stock or demiglace to just coat the pasta, duck and tasso. Continue to cook for 1 minute.

pasta (pâtes)

jolie blon pasta

If there is an anthem, a song of Acadiana, it's Jolie Blon. This song tells the story of a beautiful blonde, of loss, of unrequited love, of another man, of woe and intrigue. You just can't go wrong with a story like that. In this recipe, the rotini and Alfredeaux invoke a feeling of beautiful, curly blonde hair. Hence the name Jolie Blon Pasta.

serves 4-6

alfredeaux sauce

- 1 stick unsalted butter
- 2 cups heavy cream
- 1 toe garlic, crushed
- 1 cup grated Parmesan cheese
- 1½ cups grated Gruyère cheese

1. In a saucepan over low heat, melt the butter. **2.** Add the cream and garlic and simmer for 3 minutes. **3.** Add the Parmesan and Gruyère and whisk until heated through. Set aside.

pasta

- 1 teaspoon kosher salt
- 2 toes garlic, smashed
- 6 cups (16 ounces) rotini pasta

1. Bring 2 quarts of water to a boil. Add the salt and garlic toes. Add the pasta and cook until just cooked through, about 8 minutes. **2.** Drain and add to the crawfish and tasso sauté (recipe below).

crawfish and tasso sauté

- 2 tablespoons butter
- 4 tablespoons olive oil
- 2 toes garlic, thinly sliced
- 1 pound crawfish tails
- 1 tablespoon lemon juice
- 4 ounces Tasso (recipe on page 31), diced

1. In a large sauté pan, combine the butter and oil and cook until lightly smoking. **2.** Add the garlic; sauté for 30 seconds. **3.** Add the crawfish, lemon juice and tasso, and cook over medium heat for 1 minute. **4.** Add the prepared pasta. Continue to cook for 1 minute. **5.** Add the alfredeaux and just heat through.

Plate the pasta, and crawfish and tasso sauté. Top with alfredeaux sauce and serve.

pasta (pâtes) (**109**)

Plate and serve topped with chopped parsley.

madame CHIFFONADE
(RAG PASTA)

serves 4

This rustic dish is one I would imagine having in old New Orleans' Italian Quarter. It doesn't require any fancy pasta-making equipment, just fresh seafood. That's what makes this entree spectacular, so make sure you track down the freshest catch available.

pasta dough

- 4 eggs
- 3 cups flour

1. Place the eggs and 1 cup flour in a food processor and pulse until just mixed. Continue to add flour, about 3-4 tablespoons at a time, until the dough is very soft and slightly sticky. 2. Turn the dough out unto a floured surface and knead for about 2 minutes. 3. Wrap the dough in plastic wrap and allow it to rest for 15 minutes at room temperature. 4. On a floured surface, roll the dough out very thin and cut or tear into "rags". 5. Bring a pot of lightly salted water to a boil. Add rags and boil the pieces in salted water until just cooked through, 2-3 minutes. Strain and add to the shrimp and oysters (recipe follows).

shrimp and oysters

- 4 tablespoons butter
- 2 teaspoons black pepper
- 2 teaspoons salt
- 2 tablespoons packed fresh sage leaves
- 1 teaspoon paprika
- 1 tablespoon Worcestershire sauce
- 4 toes garlic, sliced
- 1 pound 26-30-count shrimp, peeled and deveined
- ½ cup heavy cream
- 12 gulf oysters with oyster liquor
- Juice of 1 lemon
- ½ cup chopped fresh parsley, to garnish

1. In a large sauté pan, melt the butter. 2. Add the black pepper, salt, sage, paprika, Worcestershire sauce and garlic. Cook for 1 minute. 3. Add the shrimp and sauté for 2 minutes. 4. Add the cream and oyster liquor. Cook for 1 minute. 5. Add the oysters and lemon juice and cook for 1 minute. 6. Add the pasta and continue to cook for 1 minute or until the oysters begin to lightly curl around the edges. Adjust seasoning, to taste.

chapter 7

MEATS (VIANDE)
SWEEPING AND MAJESTIC ARCS OF SWAMP COWS

What can I say about the big meats: chicken, duck, beef and pork? You will find them in classic south Louisiana dishes, from the Cajun country's brown jambalayas, gumbos and succulent sausages, to the Italians' pastas and sophisticated Creole offerings.

Let's start with my favorite protein. Pigs are big in south Louisiana. Pork is stuffed into intestines and smoked to make andouille, or combined with thyme, garlic, rice, liver and the trinity to create boudin. It is rubbed with tasso seasoning, cured or smoked to make cochon. Big chunks are slow cooked until they fall apart. They are shredded, drenched in gravy and served on big slabs of French bread for Debis po'boys, or dropped on a mountain of garlic smashed potatoes for Monreauxvias. Double-cut chops marinated in extra-virgin olive oil, herbs and seasonings are thrown on the grill and topped with kumquat and fig compote, which pretty much kicks ass. The pig is a noble animal, noble and delicious.

I can tell you of my cousin's pet pig, Sylvester. He was both loved and loathed, depending upon whom you asked. His pen was along the side of the house next to the bayou. He was a massive white male who loved to have a garden hose turned on him. The pig that is, not my cousin. Sylvester would go on walks, my cousin maintaining a death grip on the leash. Sylvester set the course as a drunken sailor might, full steam ahead and damn the torpedoes, swerving through neighbors' flower beds, careening through their gardens, plowing through their clotheslines and daintily eating their underwear. I will, for reasons of brevity, save the story of the full-but-short life and porcine times of Sylvester for another day. He was a good pig...

And poultry? For a time, my family had a nanny. Miss Lucy was an older black lady, thin, with milky green eyes and graying hair pulled back taut. Her clothes were well worn but immaculate. She lived down the street and came in to help mom with the housework, cooking and to a certain extent, my culinary education.

Miss Lucy would often bring in freshly killed fowl for dinner. Scalding and pulling at the feathers, she would deftly dress the bird. She would pop the buckshot out of dinner's legs and breast utilizing the tip of a well-worn paring knife. She always kept that knife in the left pocket of her heavily starched and impossibly white apron. Miss Lucy would make short work of it, often singing in a language that sounded French, but not the French my grandfather spoke. It was a French-African-English patois. I can still hear her songs, containing a rough beauty, but fainter now as the years progress. For the life of me, I can't describe the songs to you other than to say they were from some other, distant place.

The cow. I can tell you about the time a herd of cattle broke free from the farm down the road and blew through our yard like a hurricane, destroying almost everything in their path. The herd, pissed off, suddenly made a sweeping and majestic arc off into the swamp. I think there are still some left back behind the house. Now wild and feral, these swamp cows would bellow out at midnight, stomping alligators and eating monkey grass, descendants of the initial stampeding bovine perpetrators. Yet another story for another day.

All of these things influence the way I cook at Zydeco's. It is a culmination of whacky and sublime events and it affects how I approach a dish. It's what south Louisiana was to a young man and a big part of who and what I am today.

Spoon the bearnaise sauce over the steaks and serve with a hearty side such as roasted red potatoes.

beef tenderloin
AU POIVRE PIQUANT
WITH BÉARNAISE ROUGE

A New Orleans version of the classic Steak au Poivre. Here, we add earthy thyme to the black pepper to create a more flavorful crust. Normally a béarnaise is made with white wine and is served with fish, but this version uses red and pairs better with beef.

béarnaise rouge

- 6 egg yolks
- 2 sticks butter
- ½ cup minced red onion
- 1 cup cabernet sauvignon
- 2 teaspoons tarragon
- Juice of 1 lemon
- Pinch kosher salt
- Pinch black pepper
- Pinch garlic powder

1. Place the egg yolks in a food processor and turn it to high speed. **2.** While the motor is running and the egg yolks are whisking, melt the butter in a small saucepan until it is very hot (but do not brown). **3.** In a separate saucepan, cook the red onion in the wine with 1 teaspoon tarragon until all but a few tablespoonfuls of the wine have evaporated. **4.** With the motor running, slowly pour the hot butter in with the egg yolks. Allow this to process for 1 minute. Slowly add the red onion/cabernet mixture and the lemon juice. Process for 1 minute. **5.** Season with salt, pepper, garlic powder and the remaining 1 teaspoon tarragon.

beef tenderloin

- ¼ cup coarse-ground black pepper
- 2 tablespoons dried thyme leaves
- 1 tablespoon cayenne pepper
- 1 tablespoon paprika
- 1 teaspoon kosher salt
- 4 6-8-ounce center-cut beef tenderloin steaks
- 2 tablespoons butter
- 2 tablespoons extra-virgin olive oil

1. In a small bowl, mix the seasonings (black pepper, thyme, cayenne, paprika and salt). **2.** Press one side of each of the tenderloins into the spice mixture. **3.** In a large sauté pan, melt the butter and olive oil until lightly smoking. **4.** Place the tenderloins, seasoned side down, in the hot pan. Cook for 4 minutes, until a crust forms. Flip and cook an additional 2 minutes (for medium-rare). **5.** Remove the steaks from the pan and rest for 5 minutes.

serves 4

On each of 4 serving plates, place a lamb chop. Add a large spoonful of both the slaw and grilled eggplant. Drizzle with orange reduction and serve.

pecan-encrusted CRAWFISH AND GRUYÈRE-STUFFED LAMB CHOPS
WITH ORANGE REDUCTION, MIRLITON SLAW AND GRILLED EGGPLANT

Taking a cue from the French Trout Almondine, this New Orleans variation pairs fresh crawfish and lamb with pecans, a nut readily available in the area. The texture of the fried pecans may surprise you as it is more creamy than crunchy, and offers an indulgent, fatty mouthfeel.

crawfish and cheese stuffing

- ½ cup chopped precooked crawfish tail meat
- 1 cup shredded Gruyère cheese
- ½ teaspoon black pepper
- ½ teaspoon granulated garlic
- Juice of ½ lemon

1. Combine all of the stuffing ingredients and set aside.

lamb chops

- 1 cup chopped pecans
- ¼ cup fresh parsley, chopped
- 2 teaspoons dried rosemary
- ½ teaspoon paprika
- 1 toe garlic, minced
- ¼ cup French bread crumbs (recipe for Frech Bread Croutons on page 39)
- 2 teaspoons black pepper
- 4 lamb chops
- Crawfish and Cheese Stuffing (recipe above)
- 1 cup Creole mustard

1. Preheat oven to 350 degrees. **2.** In a large mixing bowl, combine all of the lamb chop ingredients, except the lamb, stuffing and Creole mustard, in a food processor and lightly pulse. Transfer to a shallow bowl or platter. **3.** Cut a slit in the side of each lamb chop, forming a pocket. Divide the crawfish and cheese stuffing into 4 equal portions and fill each pocket with a portion. Put a toothpick in place to hold the stuffed lamb chops closed. **4.** Coat each lamb chop in Creole mustard. Roll the chops in the pecan mixture. **5.** Place all of the chops in a black cast-iron skillet over medium-high heat and brown the meat for 2 minutes on each side. **6.** Finish cooking the meat by putting the pan in the 350-degree oven for 25-30 minutes, or until the chops reach an internal temperature of 155 degrees.

grilled eggplant

- 1 teaspoon salt
- 1 teaspoon black pepper
- 1 teaspoon dried thyme leaves
- 1 large eggplant, peeled, cut into ¼-inch slices
- Olive oil, as needed

1. Preheat an outdoor grill to medium-high heat. **2.** Combine the seasonings (salt, pepper and thyme) in a small bowl. **3.** Coat the eggplant slices in olive oil and then dip in the seasonings. **4.** Grill the eggplant on both sides until tender, about 5 minutes. Reserve.

orange reduction

- 5 cups orange juice
- 2 tablespoons sugar

1. In a saucepan over medium-high heat, simmer until the orange juice and sugar reduces to 1 cup, about 30-45 minutes. Reserve.

mirliton slaw

- 3 mirlitons, peeled, seeded, grated and drained
- 1 carrot, grated
- ¼ red onion, thinly sliced
- ½ cup diced green onion
- 2 tablespoons vinegar
- 2 tablespoons mayonnaise
- 2 tablespoons sugar
- 1 teaspoon kosher salt
- 1 teaspoon black pepper
- 1 teaspoon granulated garlic
- 1 teaspoon red pepper flakes
- 1 teaspoon celery seed

1. In a large mixing bowl, gently combine all of the mirliton slaw ingredients.

serves 4

pork debris boule
WITH GARLIC POTATO SMASH
(THE MONREAUXVIA)

When our first restaurant, Zydeco's 1, opened in Monrovia, Indiana, I wanted to create something as special as the people and the town itself. I took a homemade bread boule, filled it with potatoes, topped it with slow-cooked pork and drenched the whole thing in delicious gravy, and The Monreauxvia was born. You are going to be a big hit when you present this pure comfort food to your guests.

zydeco seasoning blend

- 1 tablespoon salt
- 1 tablespoon coarse-ground black pepper
- 2 tablespoons garlic powder
- 2 tablespoons dried thyme leaves
- ½ teaspoon cayenne
- 1 tablespoon paprika

1. Combine all ingredients and set aside.

pork

- 1 3-4-pound pork shoulder
- 12 toes garlic, halved
- ½ cup Zydeco's Seasoning Blend (recipe above)
- 1 onion, peeled and halved
- 2 carrots, peeled
- 1 stalk celery
- 1 bay leaf
- 1 cup cabernet sauvignon

1. Preheat oven to 225 degrees. **2.** Using a small paring knife, cut 24 deep slits, about 2 inches apart, into the pork. Insert ½ toe garlic into each slit. **3.** Rub the seasoning blend into the outside of the pork. **4.** Transfer the pork to a casserole dish or Dutch oven. Add the remaining ingredients. **5.** Cover with a lid or aluminum foil and cook in the 225-degree oven for 10-12 hours, or until the pork shreds easily. **6.** Remove the meat from the pan and use a pair of forks to shred. **7.** Strain the remaining pork juices through a sieve and set aside for the demiglace.

demiglace*

- 6 cups Espagnole Sauce (recipe on page 17)
- Strained pork stock
- 1 sprig fresh thyme
- 1 sprig fresh parsley
- 1 bay leaf

1. Add all of the demiglace ingredients to a saucepan and bring to a boil. **2.** Reduce the heat so the contents are at a low simmer. Allow the demiglace to thicken and reduce to half the original volume (about 2 hours). **3.** Strain and set aside.

bread boules

YEAST STARTER
- 1¼ cups bread flour
- 1 tablespoon fast-acting yeast
- Pinch kosher salt
- 2 tablespoons extra-virgin olive oil
- 2½ cups water, 110 degrees

1. To make the yeast starter, in a large stainless-steel bowl, combine all of the ingredients. **2.** Cover with a kitchen towel and put in a draft-free, warm place for 15 minutes. (At the end of 15 minutes, the mixture should be bubbling.)

DOUGH
- 2½ cups bread flour, plus more to dust work surface
- Yeast Starter (recipe above)
- 1 tablespoon olive oil
- 1 egg
- 1 tablespoon water

1. Preheat oven to 375 degrees. **2.** In a medium mixing bowl, combine the flour and yeast starter and mix well.

3. Turn the dough out onto a floured work surface and knead the bread for 10 minutes. 4. Pour the oil into a large mixing bowl. Place the dough in the bowl and turn, lightly coating the dough. Cover the dough with a kitchen towel and allow it to rise in a warm place for 1 hour. 5. Cut the dough into 8 equal portions. Form each piece into a ball shape and lightly coat with the olive oil. 6. Transfer each ball onto a lightly floured baking sheet and set in a draft-free, warm place to rise for 1 hour. 7. In a separate small bowl, mix the egg and water to make an egg wash. Brush the egg wash over the top of each bread boule. 8. Bake in the 375-degree oven for 30 minutes.

garlic potato smash

2 cups garlic toes
Extra-virgin olive oil, as needed
1 teaspoon kosher salt, plus more to taste
1 teaspoon white pepper, plus more to taste
3 pounds red potatoes
2 cups half-and-half
1 tablespoon horseradish
½ pound butter, cut into small chunks

1. Preheat oven to 350 degrees. 2. In a sheet of aluminum foil, place the garlic and drizzle with olive oil, and salt and pepper, to taste. Fold up the foil and cook in the 350-degree oven for 45 minutes. Remove and smash the garlic with the back of a fork. Set aside. 3. In a large stockpot, boil the potatoes until soft or able to be easily penetrated by a toothpick, 45-50 minutes. Drain the potatoes and coarsely smash. 4. Into the potatoes, gently fold the roasted garlic, half-and-half, horseradish, butter, 1 teaspoon salt and 1 teaspoon pepper.

to plate

Fresh sage leaves, to garnish

1. To plate, cut each bread boule in half horizontally. Scoop out the interior bread. Add a heaping spoonful of the shreddded pork to each boule and drizzle with demiglace. Garnish with sage leaves and serve.

*This recipe yields about 4 cups of demiglace.

serves 8

Spoon kumquat and onion gastrique over slices of pork tenderloin and serve.

tassoed pork
TENDERLOIN AND POTATO NANOOSE
WITH ONION AND KUMQUAT GASTRIQUE

Pork is just about as popular in Indiana as it is in Louisiana, which means I just had to put this recipe on the menu. When I first made this dish a little over 10 years ago, I knew that mom's potato salad just had to go with it. For lagniappe (a little something extra), I've added a nice gastrique that pairs well with the spiciness of the pork. It has been a big hit for the past decade and I am glad to share it with you.

potato nanoose

- 2½ cups mayonnaise
- 1 teaspoon kosher salt
- 1 teaspoon black pepper
- 2 teaspoons cayenne powder
- 2 teaspoons granulated garlic
- 6 hard-boiled eggs
- 3 pounds red potatoes
- 2 tablespoons red pimento

1. In a medium mixing bowl, combine the mayonnaise, salt, pepper, cayenne and garlic. Set aside. **2.** Peel the shells from the eggs and smash them into large chunks. **3.** Fold the cooked egg chunks into the mayonnaise. **4.** Boil the potatoes until fully cooked and a toothpick easily penetrates them, about 30-40 minutes. Drain and, using a potato masher, smash into large chunks. Gently fold the mayonnaise mixture and pimento in with the potatoes. Serve warm.

pork tenderloin

- 1 5-pound pork tenderloin
- 2 cups Worcestershire sauce
- 1 tablespoon liquid smoke
- 4 cups Tasso Seasoning (recipe on page 31)

1. Place the pork tenderloin in a large plastic zipper-lock bag. Pour Worcestershire sauce and liquid smoke over the pork and seal the bag. Place the bag in a large bowl and marinate in the refrigerator overnight. **2.** Remove the pork from the marinade and pat dry. Place the pork in a clean zipper-lock plastic bag and pour in the tasso seasoning. Shake and roll the pork so that the seasoning completely covers the meat. Refrigerate for 2-3 days. **3.** On the day you plan to serve the dish, preheat the oven to 350 degrees. **4.** Remove the pork from the plastic bag and lightly brush off excess seasoning. **5.** Bake, covered with aluminum foil until the tenderloin reaches an internal temperature of 155 degrees on an instant-read thermometer (about 1½-2 hours). **6.** Move the pork to a large cutting board and let it rest for 30 minutes. **7.** Cut into slices and serve with a side of potato nanoose.

kumquat and onion gastrique

- 1 yellow onion, thinly sliced
- 18 kumquats, halved and seeded
- ¾ cup sugar
- ½ cup cabernet sauvignon
- ½ cup water
- 3 tablespoons vinegar
- 3 sage leaves

1. In a large sauté pan over medium heat, simmer all the gastrique ingredients until they reduce to a very thick syrup, about 45 minutes.

serves 6-8

Finish with a spoonful of Marchand du Vin sauce and Creole mustard drizzled around each plate

panéed meat
AND BROILED OYSTERS
WITH ROASTED BEETS, POACHED EGG AND CHÈVRE

Panéed meats is New Orleans parlé for thinly pounded, marinated, breaded meat. Cheaper cuts of beef, veal or chicken are the typical protocol, fried in butter or extra-virgin olive oil to golden brown. The roots of this dish are clearly from the French paillard. ✻ Here, we go uptown by using rib eyes, pan fried, medium-rare and topped with roasted beets and chèvre cheese. We then add a lightly poached egg, the yolk making a lovely sauce as it mixes with the chèvre and beet greens. For another rich layer of flavor, broiled oysters crown the dish. Pairing broiled oysters with beef or veal is an old-school trick but trust me, it's really amazing. A New Orleans original indeed.

beets and greens

- 2 fresh red beets with greens attached
- 2 fresh yellow beets with greens attached
- Extra-virgin olive oil, as needed
- 4 tablespoons red wine vinegar
- 1 teaspoon kosher salt
- 1 teaspoon black pepper
- ¼ cup diced onion
- 2 tablespoons butter

1. Preheat oven to 350 degrees. 2. Cut the tops off of the beets and remove the stems. Wash the greens under cool water, drain, dry and thinly slice. 3. Rinse and dry the beets. Put the yellow and red beets in separate ovenproof pans and drizzle with olive oil. 4. Roast in the 350-degree oven until very tender, about 1½ hours. Remove and cool. 5. Peel the beets and cut each into 6 ¼-inch-thick medallions. Drizzle with vinegar and season with ½ teaspoon salt and ½ teaspoon black pepper. Set aside. 6. In a medium sauté pan, sauté the onions in the butter for 5 minutes. 7. Add the beet greens, ½ teaspoon salt and ½ teaspoon pepper and sauté another 3 minutes. Set aside.

panéed meat

- 2 cups evaporated milk or buttermilk
- 1 egg
- 1 teaspoon salt
- 2 teaspoons black pepper
- ½ teaspoon cayenne
- 1 tablespoon hot sauce
- 4 rib eyes
- 2 cups bread crumbs
- 1 teaspoon marjoram
- 1 teaspoon basil
- 1 teaspoon thyme
- 1 teaspoon granulated garlic
- 2 tablespoons butter
- 4 tablespoons extra-virgin olive oil

1. In a medium mixing bowl, combine the milk, egg, salt, 1 teaspoon black pepper, cayenne and hot sauce. 2. Pound out the rib eyes with a meat hammer. 3. Place the meat in the milk mixture and marinate in the refrigerator for 30 minutes. 4. In a large, shallow platter mix the bread crumbs, marjoram, basil, thyme, 1 teaspoon black pepper and garlic. 5. Drain the rib eyes and dredge in the bread crumbs. 6. In a large sauté pan, heat the butter and extra-virgin olive oil until lightly smoking. 7. Panfry the rib eyes for 2 minutes per side for medium-rare. Remove and drain on paper towels.

oysters

- Butter, as needed
- Hot sauce, as needed
- Worcestershire sauce, as needed
- 1 toe garlic, very thinly sliced
- Peychaud's Bitters, as needed
- Kosher salt, as needed
- Black pepper, as needed
- 8-12 raw oysters on the half shell

1. Preheat oven broiler. 2. Place a dab of butter, dash of hot sauce, dash of Worcestershire sauce, slice of garlic, dash of Peychaud's Bitters, pinch of salt and pinch of pepper on each oyster. 3. Broil for 2-3 minutes or until the edges just begin to curl. 4. Remove the oysters from the shells and set aside.

poached eggs

- Salt
- 2 tablespoons vinegar
- 4 fresh eggs

1. Bring a small saucepan of salted water to a simmer. Add vinegar. 2. Poach the eggs until the whites have set and the yolks are still soft. 3. Remove with a slotted spoon and drain.

to plate

- Panéed Meat (recipe above)
- Fresh frisé (or other light salad greens), as needed
- Beets and Greens (recipe above)
- 8 ounces fresh chèvre
- Poached Eggs (recipe above)
- Oysters (recipe above)
- ½ cup fresh parsley
- Hot sauce, as needed
- ½ cup Marchand du Vin sauce ✻
- ¼ cup Creole mustard

1. To assemble the dish, place each rib eye on a small bed of frisé greens. 2. Layer slices of red and yellow beets, and small spoonfuls of chèvre on each rib eye, forming a stack. 3. Top each stack with a poached egg, 2-3 broiled oysters, parsley and several dashes of hot sauce. Place a small spoonful of beet greens on top.

✻ You can order Marchand du Vin sauce at zydecos.net or find a simple recipe on page 17.

† Try Zatarain's Creole mustard, available at most well-stocked grocery stores, zatarains.com, at Zydeco's 5 or on our Web site, zydecos.net

serves 4

meats (viande) (123)

Spoon the choux over the chicken and top with the leftover crumbled bacon from the sweet potato chloe.

smoked chicken
YA YA WITH CRAWFISH
MAQUE CHOUX AND SWEET POTATO CHLOE

This is a simple, smoky little chicken recipe, a variation of which is always a big hit at Zydeco's. Here, I am presenting the original version that I envisioned over a decade ago. It is one of my sentimental favorites and I think you and your guests will enjoy it as well.

chicken ya ya

- 1 cup kosher salt
- 1 cup sugar
- ½ cup Worcestershire sauce
- 1 gallon water
- 4 bone-in chicken breasts
- 4 pats butter
- 2 tablespoons dried rosemary
- 1 tablespoon granulated garlic
- 1 tablespoon coarse-ground black pepper
- 2 tablespoons paprika

1. Preheat a smoker to 250 degrees, according to the manufacturer's instructions. **2.** Make a brine solution by mixing the salt, sugar, Worcestershire and water together in a large container. **3.** Brine the chicken in the refrigerator for 6 hours. Drain and wipe the meat dry. **4.** Place back in the refrigerator, uncovered, for 2 additional hours to dry the skin. **5.** Make a small cut and slide 1 pat of butter under the skin of each chicken breast. Season the outside of each chicken breast with the rosemary, garlic, black pepper and paprika. **6.** Smoke in the 250-degree cooker until the internal temperature of the chicken reaches 165 degrees on an instant-read thermometer inserted into the thickest part of the breast (about 2-2½ hours).

sweet potato chloe

- 2 cups peeled and cubed sweet potatoes
- 4 slices smoked bacon
- 1 teaspoon thyme leaves
- ½ teaspoon red pepper flakes
- ½ teaspoon kosher salt
- Pinch allspice
- 1 teaspoon coarse-ground black pepper
- 2 tablespoons butter

1. Place the sweet potatoes in a large stockpot and cover with water. Boil until tender, about 30 minutes. Drain and set aside. **2.** In a heavy saucepan or cast-iron skillet, sauté the bacon until crisp. Remove and reserve. **3.** To the saucepan, add the sweet potatoes, thyme, red pepper flakes, salt, allspice and pepper. **4.** Brown well, about 5-7 minutes. Add the butter and set aside.

crawfish and corn maque choux

- 1 large corn on the cob (equal to 1 cup kernels)
- 4 tablespoons butter
- 1 teaspoon coarse-ground black pepper
- 1 bay leaf
- 1 toe garlic, sliced
- ½ cup diced celery
- 1 cup crawfish tails
- 1 cup heavy cream
- Pinch cayenne pepper
- Dash Tabasco sauce
- ½ teaspoon paprika

1. Scrape and remove the corn from the cob and set aside. **2.** Place 2 tablespoons of butter in a sauté pan. Add the pepper, bay leaf, garlic and celery. Sauté over medium heat for 1 minute. **3.** Add the corn and cook for 2 minutes. **4.** Add the crawfish tails and cook for 3 minutes. **5.** Lower the heat to low; add the heavy cream and cook for 7 minutes. Add 2 tablespoons of butter, a pinch of cayenne, Tabasco and paprika.

serves 4-6

To plate, place a large spoonful of red rice on the center of each serving plate. Place a piece of chicken on top of the rice and spoon the mirliton and fig sauce over the top.

chicken pontalba
WITH MIRLITON, MISSION FIGS AND RED RICE

She's had a hard life, New Orleans; a lady resolute, a fighter. The years: 2005-Katrina, 1965-"Billion Dollar" Betsy (the one I lived through as a child and even today I vividly remember), 1794 and 1788- The Great New Orleans' Fires, also unceremoniously known as "The Great Flambé," "The Reconstruction" of the late 1800s and the many other catastrophes in between, both natural and man-made. She has seen more than her share of bad times, lost some of her culture, her people. ✱ During "The Great Flambé," and while under Spanish rule, quite a bit of the original French buildings were destroyed. In their place, the Spanish style was used, including wrought-iron balconies and central courtyards. You see it in picture postcards and TV programs about Mardi Gras. You know, the ones where tipsy tourists from Topeka are dangerously close to falling to their deaths from the second floor galleries. It's what most people envision when they think of The French Quarter, Spanish architecture that is, not so much inebriated revelers from the Midwest hanging like grapes from street lamps. ✱ In the midst of one such rebuilding period long ago, the Baroness Pontalba commissioned a slew of architects to design apartment buildings to replace crumbling structures. Not liking any one design, she fired the lot of them, taking the best bits from each and creating a hybrid style which became the Pontalba Buildings that straddle the Cathedral. They contribute to the unique look and feel of the Vieux Carré. Her influence was so admired in the city a dish was named after her and is still served today at many of the finer restaurants around town. ✱ My version of the traditional New Orleans' Chicken Pontalba incorporates the Spanish, French and Creole influences just as Baroness Pontalba did when she created an architectural amalgam. This dish is easy to make, it's spicy, it's sweet, it's rich and it's earthy, and in a small way celebrates the rich diversity which gives the city its strength.

red rice

- ½ cup minced onion
- 1 tablespoon olive oil
- 1 cup long-grain rice
- 1 tablespoon butter
- ½ cup chopped pecans
- 2 cups tomato juice
- 1 cup chicken stock
- 1 tablespoon paprika
- 1 tablespoon Worcestershire sauce
- 1 tablespoon hot sauce
- 2 teaspoons salt
- 1 teaspoon pepper
- 1 cup diced Creole tomato ✱
- ½ cup diced green onion

1. In a large sauté pan, sauté the minced onion in the olive oil for 3 minutes. **2.** Add the rice, butter and pecans and cook for 3 minutes. **3.** Add all of the remaining ingredients, except the tomato and green onion, and cover. Bring the mixture to a boil and stir once. **4.** Cover and reduce the heat to medium. Simmer, stirring occasionally, until most of the liquid has cooked off and the rice is done, about 20-25 minutes. **5.** Fold in the tomato and green onion. Cook for an additional 1 minute. Reserve.

(recipe continued on page 128)

serves 6-8

(recipe continued from page 127)

chicken and sauce

- 1 whole fryer chicken, cut into 8 pieces
- 4 tablespoons extra-virgin olive oil
- 1 cup diced onion
- 1 bay leaf
- 1 cup diced green bell pepper
- 3 ancho chilies in adobo sauce, finely chopped
- 1 teaspoon paprika
- ½ teaspoon cayenne pepper
- 2 teaspoons cumin
- 2 teaspoons coriander
- 1 teaspoon black pepper
- 1 teaspoon kosher salt
- 3 toes garlic, sliced
- 2 mirlitons, peeled, seeded and cut into quarters
- 4 ounces dried mission figs, halved lengthwise
- 2 cups chicken stock
- 1 tablespoon flour
- Red Rice (recipe on page 127)

1. Preheat oven to 350 degrees. **2.** In a large, cast-iron Dutch oven, brown the chicken in the olive oil, about 3 minutes per side. **3.** Remove the cooked chicken from the pan and add the onion, bay leaf, bell pepper, ancho chilies and seasonings (paprika, cayenne, cumin, coriander, black pepper, salt and garlic). Cook for 5 minutes. **4.** Add the mirliton and figs and continue to cook for an additional 5 minutes. **5.** Return the chicken to the pot. Add the chicken stock and place in the 350-degree oven. Cook until the internal temperature of the thickest piece of chicken reaches 165 degrees, about 30 minutes. **6.** Remove the chicken from the Dutch oven and place the lid back on the Dutch oven to keep it warm. **7.** Sprinkle the flour over the top of the mirliton and fig sauce. Continue to cook uncovered on the stovetop for 10 more minutes, or until the sauce has thickened and reduced by half.

*Creole tomatoes are medium-size tomatoes native to New Orleans. Feel free to use your favorite local variety.

duck clemenceaux

I have always loved the popular dish Chicken Clemenceau. It's an old-money, sophisticated New Orleans offering created in the last century by a hotshot, big-time chef and served at fancy restaurants where you never really feel comfortable. The kind in which you know you will make some sort of embarrassing faux pas. * In this version, I've streamlined the recipe, substituted duck for the chicken and put an "x" at the end of the name. By doing all of these things (especially the addition of the "x"), I simplified the process and yet, added a complexity of flavor that makes it not so much like a stuffy city dish, but more like something you have ova by ya momma's and she doesn't care if you use the wrong fork. It's one of my all-time favorites, and it tastes more better, which is always a good thing.

serves 6-8

par-boiled potatoes

- 3 pounds new red potatoes, washed, skin on
- 3 tablespoons salt
- 1 tablespoon black pepper
- 1 tablespoon Tabasco sauce
- 1 teaspoon cayenne pepper
- ½ teaspoon liquid crab boil
- 2 bay leaves
- 1 small red onion, halved
- 1 stalk celery, halved
- 3 toes garlic, crushed

1. To a large stockpot, add the potatoes and cover with water. 2. Add all of the seasonings and bring the potatoes to a low boil. Boil the potatoes for 15 minutes. 3. Remove from heat and let them soak for 20 minutes in the seasoned water. 4. Drain and set the potatoes aside to dry.

duck clemenceaux

- 1 whole duck, cut into 8 pieces
- 4 tablespoons butter
- Par-Boiled Potatoes (see above)
- 2 cups fresh peas
- 3 toes garlic, sliced
- 1 cup dry white wine
- ½ pound fresh medium button mushrooms, thickly sliced

1. Preheat oven to 400 degrees. 2. Place the duck pieces in a large cast-iron skillet or ovenproof sauté pan and brown in the 400-degree oven for 30 minutes, flipping halfway through (at 15 minutes). Remove the duck from the pan and set aside. 3. Add the butter and par-boiled potatoes to the pan and brown, cooking for about 5 minutes. 4. Add the peas, garlic, duck and white wine; cover and cook for 15 minutes. 5. Add the mushrooms and cook for 5 minutes. Plate and serve warm.

Place the duck, carrots, onions and turnips onto a large serving platter. Spoon the Creole salpicon over the duck and vegetables. Garnish with the crumbled bacon and fresh parsley

duck abbeville
WITH CREOLE SALPICON, CARROT, ONION AND TURNIPS

Walking into my uncle's workshop in Abbeville was always fun. He had hundreds of duck decoys lining his shelves; in the rafters, on the floor, from ultra-realistic sculptures to primitives made from rough cypress blocks. ✱ Attached to the workshop was "the caboose". During the hot and humid Louisiana summers, he would cook dinner for us in the caboose's fully stocked kitchen. The smell of herbs and spices and other wonderful aromas filled the air. This duck recipe reminds me of those good times.

duck

- 1 duck
- 1 cup sugar
- 1 cup plus 1 tablespoon kosher salt
- 1 tablespoon black pepper
- 1 orange, peeled and quartered
- 1 bay leaf
- 8 ounces bacon
- 1 cup duck or chicken stock
- 1 pound whole turnips, peeled
- 1 pound carrots, peeled, halved
- 2 onions, peeled and quartered
- 4 toes garlic, crushed

1. Preheat oven to 350 degrees. 2. Remove the giblets and wing tips from the duck and rinse the body well. Save the liver for the salpicon, and the neck and giblets for a duck stock at a later date. 3. Brine the duck by placing it in a large bowl and covering with water. Add the sugar and 1 cup salt. Allow the duck to soak for 3 hours. 4. Remove, drain and pat dry. Place the duck on a plate and into the refrigerator uncovered for 1 hour to dry the skin. 5. To the outside and inside of the duck, apply 1 tablespoon salt and pepper. Place the orange pieces and bay leaf in the duck cavity. 6. In a large ovenproof stockpot or cast-iron Dutch oven, brown the bacon. Remove the bacon, crumble and set aside. 7. Place the duck in the bacon fat and brown on all sides, about 5 minutes per side. 8. To the stockpot or Dutch oven, add the stock, turnips, carrots, onions and garlic. Bring to a simmer. 9. Place the lid on the pot or Dutch oven and braise the duck in the 350-degree oven for 2 hours.

creole salpicon*

- 3 tablespoons butter
- 3 tablespoons flour
- 3 cups milk
- Pinch allspice
- Pinch granulated garlic
- ½ teaspoon salt
- 6-8 black peppercorns
- Sprig fresh parsley, plus more to garnish
- Sprig fresh thyme
- ⅛ teaspoon nutmeg
- 2 Creole tomatoes, peeled and diced
- 1 cup diced mushrooms
- Duck liver (reserved above), chopped
- 1 cup U26-30-count shrimp, chopped
- 1 cup diced ham
- Duck (recipe above)

1. In a small saucepan, make a roux by cooking the butter and flour over medium heat, whisking continuously, for 3 minutes. 2. Add the milk, allspice, garlic, salt, peppercorns, parsley, thyme and nutmeg and cook, whisking often, for 15 minutes. 3. Pour the mixture through a sieve into a separate medium saucepan. Add the tomato, mushrooms, duck liver, shrimp and ham and cook for 5 minutes.

*A salpicon is the French technique of binding a sauce with diced or chopped ingredients. In this salpicon, shrimp, duck liver, mushrooms, tomatoes and ham are incorporated into a béchamel.

serves 4-6

chapter 8

Millions of tons of sugar are produced each year in Louisiana. In fact, some of it might end up in these desserts.

RAISING CANE

In the fall, drive down Highway 90 and LA 1 between Des Allemands and Thibodaux, and make sure your windows are rolled down. As you drive, on either side of the road, you'll notice large piles of green and brown sugarcane stacked up to the sky. Massive, battered harvesters squat and waddle across and parallel to rows of cane. They sprout rotating spiral blades and slash miles and miles of the multi-jointed batons. On the sides of the fields, menacing metallic, articulated hydraulic fingers pull at the piles of the freshly clipped cane and drop it into large wheeled cages attached to diesel trucks. These trucks make endless roundtrips, hauling the slashed and plucked cane to the sugar refinery in Raceland.

You notice that fires dot the landscape. They are set on purpose, burning off the leaves and releasing a thick, sweet smoke. Your car cuts through the smoked-sugar haze as you continue to drive southwest towards Thibodaux. Make sure your windows are rolled down and breathe the swirling smoke in deep. It's like breathing in an ethereal dessert.

Drive through Raceland and you see the piles of white granulated sugar pushed to and fro by frantic bulldozers. You will see large rusty pipes spew bagasse, the cane pulp, high into the air and into large mountains. The bagasse is destined for furnaces where it will be burned, boiling the sugarcane juice into sticky syrup. The sweet smell hangs over the town and stays with you and in your car all the way to Thibodaux.

Before the Civil War, Louisiana produced most of the sugar found in kitchens all over the United States. Today, sugar is still one of the driving forces of the Louisiana economy. It's cheap and plentiful and used in some very famous southern desserts and beverages. Sugary stacked Napoleons filled with fresh fruit, the doberge, the raisin bread puddings, the pecan pies, the cakes and confections in and around the entire Gulf Coast are all made from this cane sugar.

Millions of tons of sugar are produced every year in Louisiana. In fact, some of it will end up in these desserts. Marry a not-so-miniature pile of the sugar, milk, fruit and French bread for a south Louisiana bread pudding. Blend it with chocolate and almond to create a doberge. If there is a better cake to enjoy with friends and family, I can't think of one. Push the sugar around with eggs, cane syrup and pecans for a sinful pecan pie. It's as if you are driving down to Thibodaux during fall cane harvest and the smoky sugar clouds are all around you.

Dust with powdered sugar and enjoy.

beignets
WITH CAFÉ AU LAIT

The single most requested item at Zydeco's is probably the beignet. This simple doughnut has close ties to the Crescent City. They are very easy to make and yours can be as good as any in New Orleans. ✱ Although any coffee can be enjoyed with beignets, coffee and chicory would be my choice. The story goes that during the Civil War, chicory was added to coffee to extend the scarce commodity. Today, it is still produced by coffee companies and is extremely popular throughout south Louisiana. A milder variation, very popular in eastern Acadiana, mixes equal parts brewed coffee and chicory with warmed milk. The mix is known as "coffee milk."

beignets (new orleans fried doughnuts)

½ cup milk
½ cup water
1 egg
3 cups flour
1 tablespoon baking powder
Pinch kosher salt
Powdered sugar, as needed

1. Preheat a deep fryer to 350 degrees. 2. In a medium mixing bowl, combine the milk, water and egg. 3. In a separate medium mixing bowl, combine the flour, baking powder and salt. 4. Stir the dry ingredients into the wet ingredients. 5. Gently knead the dough, but do not overwork it (approximately 3 minutes). Measure the dough into 4-ounce balls. On a lightly floured work surface, roll out each ball into a 3"x 5" rectangle, ⅛-¼-inch thick. 6. Fry the rectangles in the 350-degree oil, in batches if necessary, for 2 minutes per side. Remove to a paper towel-lined plate to drain.

café au lait (coffee milk)

½ cup prepared coffee and chicory ✱
½ cup warmed milk

1. Combine the ingredients and serve with the beignets.

✱ Hutch recommends New Orleans Blend Coffee and Chicory Ground by Community Coffee. communitycoffee.com This blend is also available at Zydeco's 5 or zydecos.net

serves 6

Serve cold with a dollop of chicory whipped cream, fresh mint leaves and a pot of hot coffee

pecan pie WITH COFFEE AND CHICORY WHIPPED CREAM

Pecans are plentiful in the south. Where I grew up, along the swamps of Magnolia Ridge, my family's property included an old pecan grove. The trees were planted by a distant relative, and produced an abundance of nuts, meaning fresh pecan pies and pralines were always on the table, and almost taken for granted. My brother and I would climb the trees and shake the limbs, making the pecans rain down onto the moss-covered ground. Today, it's somewhat easier to acquire pecans and easier yet to make this pie.

serves 8

pâte brisée (basic crust)

2 cups flour
1 stick (¼ pound) butter, sliced into pats and frozen
Pinch salt
½ cup cold water

1. Place 1½ cups flour in a food processor. Add the butter and salt, and pulse on and off. **2.** Add the chilled water and pulse on and off again. **3.** Sprinkle the remaining ½ cup flour on a clean work surface. Turn dough out onto the lightly floured area. Form and lightly press the dough into a ball, then flatten it out slightly to make a disk. (Do not knead or overwork the dough.) **4.** Wrap the dough ball in wax paper and allow it to rest for 30 minutes. **5.** Roll the dough out to ¼-inch thickness and place in a nonstick 9-inch pie pan. **6.** Work your way around the rim of the pie pan, pressing the back of a fork into the pastry to create a decorative edge. Trim off the excess and set aside.

coffee and chicory whipped cream

½ pint heavy cream
1 tablespoon Kahlua coffee liqueur
½ teaspoon almond extract
2 tablespoons sugar
½ tablespoon instant coffee and chicory *

1. Place all of the whipped cream ingredients into a food processor and blend for 3-5 minutes, or until soft peaks form. **2.** Set aside until you're ready to plate the pie.

filling

2 cups chopped pecans
1 9-inch Pâte Brisée (recipe above)
5 eggs
1 cup Steen's 100% Pure Cane Syrup +
1 cup sugar
¾ cup brown sugar
1 tablespoon cornstarch
½ teaspoon vanilla extract
½ teaspoon almond extract
1 tablespoon bourbon
Pinch salt
2 tablespoons butter
Coffee and Chicory Whipped Cream (recipe above), to serve
Fresh mint, to garnish

1. Preheat oven to 450 degrees. **2.** Add the chopped pecans to the prepared pâte brisée and set aside. **3.** In the bowl of a food processor, mix the eggs until they are as smooth as possible, about 3 minutes. **4.** Add all of the remaining ingredients, except the whipped cream and mint, into the food processor and continue to whisk for 1 minute. Pour the pie filling over the pecans. **5.** Bake the pie in the 450-degree oven for 15 minutes. Reduce the heat to 350 degrees and bake for an additional 30-35 minutes, or until the filling has just set. Remove the pie from the oven, allow it to cool and refrigerate. **6.** When you're ready to serve, cut the pie into 8 equal slices.

* Hutch recommends New Orleans Blend Coffee and Chicory Ground by Community Coffee. communitycoffee.com. This blend is also available at Zydeco's 5 or zydecos.net

+ You can purchase Steen's online at steensyrup.com, zydecos.net, or at Zydeco's 5.

Spoon the bananas and rum syrup over the doberge slices and sprinkle with pecans.

chocolate + coffee
DOBERGE WITH DRUNKEN RUM BANANAS AND PECANS (NEW ORLEANS DOUGH-BEARJ)

They stream out of a claustrophobic Tulane classroom, down four flights of wide, wooden and well-worn stairs. The students and professor pass by corkboards festooned with stern academic notices and scrawled flyers announcing apartments for rent, all held in place with a thousand staples and pins. They walk together through dusty, ancient and dry academic air. The group presses down endless dimly lit, musky corridors and finally through Gibson Hall's massive doors, into a cool and clear Crescent City night. Laughing now and with the sense of a heavy weight lifting up and off of their shoulders, a certain lightness is felt in each and every step. Another class successfully completed; now for a little relaxation. One of the more astute among us calls our gathering "study hall". * The group slides past moss-laden oaks and purple azaleas, down St. Charles Avenue and toward the river. To the left, Audubon Park and Magazine Street. Just ahead, their destination. It is a tiny, unpainted shotgun house converted into a coffee shop. Tucked away and to the right, off the avenue, entangled in streams of mirliton ivy and well hidden, it is as if it grew up and out of the rich delta mud. * They all stream through light cypress French doors and pull large, round tables together. The study hall commences with the ordering of small cups of stupidly strong coffee. A flask is produced, filled with a thick, sweet dark rum. It is offered up by one of the more attentive participants and accepted by all. Overhead, a verdigris fan is gyrating slowly; its orbit dangerously skewed and out of balance as if attempting to shove through a viscous liquid. The eccentric and warped wooden blades are pushing the night air in and around the gathering. An astute visitor to the city once wrote that New Orleans is the northern most Caribbean city. Tonight, that distinction feels well deserved. * Within these walls, the problems of the world are revealed, discussed and easily solved by everyone and all. More importantly for this story, orders are placed for doberge. If there were a better confection to be served at that moment, no one could think of one. * That professor always thinks fondly of years teaching and of his students. Those were the days of impromptu caffeinated study halls in intimate smoke-filled coffee houses. There, one could find small shots of dark rum poured into demitasse and of sweet squares of dense, layered doberge served up on an endless stream of porcelain plates. * Today, that professor is in the back with his Ph.D. hanging over the deep fat fryers, sharing a bit of his old professorial days with you. It's a small taste of that coffee house, the animated conversations, the doberge and of those easy New Orleans nights. Doberge is so common within The City and is, much to my chagrin, almost nonexistent elsewhere. Let's fix that now.

doberge batter

Butter or cooking spray, as needed
4 cups flour plus more, as needed
1 tablespoon baking powder
Pinch kosher salt
3 1-ounce squares unsweetened chocolate
2 sticks butter
3 cups sugar
6 eggs, separated, whites beaten until stiff
2 cups buttermilk
3 tablespoons amaretto liqueur
1 teaspoon vanilla extract

1. Preheat oven to 350 degrees. Grease and flour 2 9" x 3" round springform cake pans. **2.** In a small mixing bowl, combine the 4 cups flour, baking powder and kosher salt. **3.** Melt the chocolate in the top of a bain-marie or double boiler. **4.** In a food processor, cream the butter and sugar. Add the egg yolks, flour mixture, buttermilk, amaretto, vanilla extract and melted chocolate. Mix well, running the food processor for about 1 minute. **5.** Pour the batter into a large bowl and gently fold in the beaten egg whites. **6.** Divide and pour the batter into the springform cake pans. Bake in the 350-degree oven for 45 minutes or until the cakes reach 190 degrees in the center. **7.** Allow the cakes to cool completely. Carefully cut each cake horizontally into thirds, making 6 rounds.

(recipe continued on page 140)

(recipe continued from page 139)

doberge filling

- 1 cup sugar
- 3 tablespoons instant dark roast coffee
- 4 tablespoons cornstarch
- ½ cup flour
- 3 squares semisweet chocolate
- 2 12-ounce cans evaporated milk
- 10 egg yolks, whisked
- 2 tablespoons butter
- 1½ ounces (1 shot) amaretto liqueur
- 1 tablespoon coffee liqueur
- ½ tablespoon vanilla extract

1. In a large mixing bowl, combine the sugar, coffee, cornstarch and flour. **2.** In a small saucepan over low heat, melt together the chocolate and milk. **3.** Add the chocolate milk to the flour/sugar mixture and stir well. Return the mixture to the saucepan and continue to cook over medium heat, whisking continuously. **4.** Slowly add the egg yolks and continue to whisk. **5.** Cook over medium heat, whisking continuously for 3-5 minutes or until very thick. **6.** Remove the mixture from the heat and add the butter, amaretto, coffee liqueur and vanilla. Pour into a bowl, cover with plastic wrap and cool completely.

doberge frosting

- 6 cups sugar
- 1 12-ounce can evaporated milk
- 3 ounces unsweetened chocolate
- 1 tablespoon instant dark roast coffee
- ½ stick butter
- 1 teaspoon vanilla extract
- 1½ cups crushed espresso beans

1. Combine the sugar and milk in a heavy saucepan and bring to 195 degrees, stirring constantly. Reduce the heat to low and simmer for 5 minutes without stirring. **2.** Blend in the chocolate, coffee, butter and vanilla, cooking 1 minute more. **3.** Remove the frosting from the heat and pour into a bowl; cool completely. **4.** Beat the frosting well and apply to the doberges. Press the crushed espresso beans into the top of the cakes.

drunken bananas and pecans

- 1 stick plus 4 tablespoons butter
- 1 cup broken pecans
- Pinch kosher salt
- ½ cup brown sugar
- ½ cup cane sugar
- 1 teaspoon allspice
- 8 bananas, peeled and halved lengthwise
- 1 cup dark rum

1. In a small sauté pan, melt 4 tablespoons butter. Add the pecans and salt and sauté until browned, about 1-2 minutes. Set aside. **2.** In a large sauté pan, melt the remaining butter, brown sugar and cane sugar (3-5 minutes). **3.** Add the allspice and bananas. Cook over medium heat for 3 minutes, stirring gently. **4.** Remove from heat and add the dark rum.

serves 8

blueberry
AND WHITE CHOCOLATE
BREAD PUDDING WITH CHAMBORD SAUCE

I was sort of burned out on the traditional raisin bread pudding in rum sauce, so I decided to give my recipe a much-needed change. At the time, blueberries happened to be in season and I got my hands on some that were beautiful and plump. Now what to pair with the berries? I have never liked chocolate bread pudding. The chocolate always seemed to throw off the balance of the dessert. I felt as though I was being bludgeoned by a screaming chocolate sledgehammer. But what about white chocolate? There was an idea. Mild and smooth, white chocolate would complement the blueberries and not overpower them. Blueberry and white chocolate bread pudding was born and it was an instant hit!

serves 8

chambord sauce

- 1 stick butter
- ½ cup sugar
- 1 egg
- 1½ ounces (1 shot) Chambord

1. In the top of a bain-marie, melt the butter. **2.** Add the sugar and whisk slowly for 3 minutes. Slowly add the egg; stir rapidly so as not to scramble. Cook for another 3 minutes, whisking slowly. **3.** Remove the bain-marie from the heat and whisk in the Chambord.

Yields about 1 cup sauce

bread pudding

- 3 cups milk
- 2½ cups bread crumbs
- 3 eggs
- 1½ cups sugar
- 1 tablespoon vanilla extract
- 1 cup white chocolate morsels
- 2 cups fresh blueberries
- 1 cup Chambord Sauce (recipe above)
- ¼ cup powdered sugar

1. Preheat oven to 350 degrees. **2.** In a large mixing bowl, combine the milk, bread crumbs, eggs, sugar and vanilla extract. Allow this mix to rest for 10 minutes. Fold in the white chocolate and 1½ cups blueberries. **3.** Pour the bread pudding batter into a greased 7" x 10" brownie pan. Bake in the 350-degree oven for 1 hour. **4.** Remove from the oven and allow the bread pudding to cool for 1 hour. **5.** To remove the bread pudding, invert the pan on a large plate and cut into slices. Distribute the Chambord sauce evenly onto each of 8 serving plates. Carefully place a serving of bread pudding on top of the sauce on each plate and dust with powdered sugar.

INDEX

A
Absinthe, **53**

Alphreadeaux, **17**

Andouille, **23**

Andouille and Potato Galette with Braised Cabbage, **47**

B
Back to Basics

The Trinity, **13**

Mirepoix, **13**

Basic Roux, **14**

Stock Facile (easy stock), **15**

Brown Stock, **15**

Duck Stock, **15**

Shrimp Stock, **15**

Hollandaise, **16**

Mayonnaise, **16**

Crawfish Sauce a la Thibodaux, **16**

Remoulade, **16**

Jus Lie (simple sauce), **17**

Alphreadeaux, **17**

Espagnole Sauce, **17**

Marchand de vin Sauce (the wine merchant's sauce), **17**

Béchamel, **17**

Bordelaise a la Mouvrelle Onleans, **17**

Béarnaise Rouge (red béarnaise), **18**

Meuniere, **18**

Zydeco's Shrimp Sauté, **18**

Basic Roux, **14**

Béarnaise Rouge (red béarnaise), **18**

Béchamel, **17**

Beef Tenderloin Au Poivre Piquant with Béarnaise Rouge, **115**

Beignet L'ecrevisse, **89**

Beignets with Café Au Lait, **135**

Blackened Crab Cakes in a Nest, **105**

Blackened Red Snapper with Chipotle Aioli, Tiger Shrimp Creole Sauce and Hammered Brussels Sprouts, **77**

Blueberry and White Chocolate Bread Pudding with Chambord Sauce, **141**

Bordelaise a la Mouvrelle Onleans, **17**

Boudin, **25**

Boutte Alliator Sausage, **29**

Broiled Frog Legs with Crab Ravigote, Asparagus and Creole Tomato, **45**

Brown Stock, **15**

Buffaleaux Wings with Creole Cream Cheese and Pickled Mirliton, **97**

C
Café Nouvelle Orleans, **44**

Catfish Pecandine and Dirty Rice with Blood Orange Olive and Red Onion Salad, **69**

Chaurice, **27**

Cherry Bounce, **53**

Chicken Pontalba with Mirliton, Mission Figs and Red Rice, **127**

Chocolate and Coffee Doberge with Drunken Rum Bananas and Pecans, **139**

Crab, Artichoke and Garlic Pizza, **87**

Crawfish Boil, **83**

Crawfish Pie, **59**

Crawfish Sauce a la Thibodaux, **16**

Crawfish Tasso and Chaurice Omelet with Shredded Pepper Jack Cheese, **37**

D
Desserts

Beignets with Café Au Lait, **135**

Pecan Pie with Coffee and Chicory Whipped Cream, **137**

Chocolate and Coffee Doberge with Drunken Rum Bananas and Pecans, **139**

Blueberry and White Chocolate Bread Pudding with Chambord Sauce, **141**

Duck Abbeville with Creole Salpicon, Carrot, Onion and Turnips, **131**

Duck and Andouille Jambalaya, **101**

Duck Clemenceaux, **129**

Duck Stock, **15**

E
Espagnole Sauce, **17**

F
Fat Tuesday

Crawfish Boil, **83**

Les Chevrettes Boucane Boutte (BBQ Shrimp), **85**

Crab, Artichoke and Garlic Pizza, **87**

Beignet L'ecrevisse, **89**

Muffulettas with Gaufrettes, **93**

Peacemakers with Horseradish Aioli, **95**

Buffaleaux Wings with Creole Cream Cheese and Pickled Mirliton, **97**

Oreilles Sales (Pigs Ears 3 Ways), **99**

Duck and Andouille Jambalaya, **101**

Fried "Bustah" Crabs with Tomato and Avocado Remoulade, **71**

Fish and Seafood
Catfish Pecandine and Dirty Rice with Blood Orange Olive and Red Onion Salad, **69**

Fried "Bustah" Crabs with Tomato and Avocado Remoulade, **71**

Shrimp Baronne, **73**

Speckled Trout Stuffed with Catfish, **75**

Blackened Red Snapper with Chipotle Aioli, Tiger Shrimp Creole Sauce and Hammered Brussels Sprouts, **77**

G
German Coast Boudin with Onions, Beer and Creole Mustard Pan Sauce, **41**

Golden Alligator Sauce Piquant, **57**

H
Hollandaise, **16**

Hurricane, **51**

J
Jolie Blon Pasta, **109**

Jus Lie (simple sauce), **17**

L
Les Chevrettes Boucane Boutte (BBQ Shrimp), **85**

Lost Bread, **49**

M

Madame Chiffonade (Rag Pasta), **111**

Marchand de vin Sauce (the wine merchant's sauce), **17**

Mayonnaise, **16**

Meats

Beef Tenderloin Au Poivre Piquant with Béarnaise Rouge, **115**

Pecan-Encrusted Crawfish and Gruyère-Stuffed Lamb Chops with Orange Reduction Mirliton Slaw and Grilled Eggplant, **117**

Pork Debris Boule with Garlic Potato Smash (The Monreauxvia), **118**

Tassoed Pork Tenderloin and Potato Nanoose with Onion and Kumquat Gastrique, **121**

Panéed Meat and Broiled Oysters with Roasted Beets, Poached Egg and Chevre, **123**

Smoked Chicken Ya Ya with Crawfish Maque Choux and Sweet Potato Chloe, **125**

Chicken Pontalba with Mirliton, Mission Figs and Red Rice, **127**

Duck Clemenceaux, **129**

Duck Abbeville with Creole Salpicon, Carrot, Onion and Turnips, **131**

Meuniere, **18**

Mirepoix, **13**

Muffulettas with Gaufrettes, **93**

N

North Shore Duck and Tasso Pasta, **107**

O

Old Square

Golden Alligator Sauce Piquant, **57**

Crawfish Pie, **59**

Red Beans and Rice with Sausage, **61**

Seafood Gumbo, **63**

Shrimp Creole, **65**

Oreilles Sales (Pigs Ears 3 Ways), **99**

Oyster and Chicken Liver En Brochette with Sweet Mirliton Spears and New Orleans Bordelaise (Angels and Devils on Horseback), **39**

P

Panéed Meat and Broiled Oysters with Roasted Beets, Poached Egg and Chevre, **123**

Pasta

Blackened Crab Cakes in a Nest, **105**

North Shore Duck and Tasso Pasta, **107**

Jolie Blon Pasta, **109**

Madame Chiffonade (Rag Pasta), **111**

Peacemakers with Horseradish Aioli, **95**

Pecan-Encrusted Crawfish and Gruyère-Stuffed Lamb Chops with Orange Reduction Mirliton Slaw and Grilled Eggplant, **117**

Pecan Pie with Coffee and Chicory Whipped Cream, **137**

Pickled Meats, **33**

Pork Debris Boule with Garlic Potato Smash (The Monreauxvia), **118**

R

Red Beans and Rice with Sausage, **61**

Remoulade, **16**

S

Sausages and Seasoning Meats

Andouille, **23**

Boudin, **25**

Chaurice, **27**

Boutte Alligator Sausage, **29**

Tasso, **31**

Pickled Meats, **33**

Sazerac, **51**

Seafood Gumbo, **63**

Shrimp Baronne, **73**

Shrimp Creole, **65**

Shrimp Sauté with Fried Grit Cakes and Béchamel Sauce, **43**

Shrimp Stock, **15**

Smoked Chicken Ya Ya with Crawfish Maque Choux and Sweet Potato Chloe, **125**

Speckled Trout Stuffed with Catfish, **75**

Stock Facile (easy stock), **15**

Sunday Brunch

Crawfish Tasso and Chaurice Omelet with Shredded Pepper Jack Cheese, **37**

Oyster and Chicken Liver En Brochette with Sweet Mirliton Spears and New Orleans Bordelaise (Angels and Devils on Horseback), **39**

German Coast Boudin with Onions, Beer and Creole Mustard Pan Sauce, **41**

Shrimp Sauté with Fried Grit Cakes and Béchamel Sauce, **43**

Café Nouvelle Orleans, **44**

Broiled Frog Legs with Crab Ravigote, Asparagus and Creole Tomato, **45**

Andouille and Potato Galette with Braised Cabbage, **47**

Lost Bread, **49**

Sazerac, **51**

Hurricane, **51**

Cherry Bounce, **53**

Absinthe, **53**

T

Tasso, **31**

Tassoed Pork Tenderloin and Potato Nanoose with Onion and Kumquat Gastrique, **121**

The Trinity, **13**

Z

Zydeco's Shrimp Sauté, **18**

index **143**

www.ingramcontent.com/pod-product-compliance
Lightning Source LLC
LaVergne TN
LVRC091354060526
838201LV00042B/414